MULTINATIONAL DISTRIBUTION

MULTINATIONAL DISTRIBUTION

Channel, Tax, and Legal Strategies

R. Duane Hall
Ralph J. Gilbert

PRAEGER SPECIAL STUDIES • PRAEGER SCIENTIFIC

New York • Philadelphia • Eastbourne, UK
Toronto • Hong Kong • Tokyo • Sydney

Library of Congress Cataloging in Publication Data

Hall, R. Duane.
  Multinational distribution.

  Includes index.
  1. Export sales. 2. Foreign trade regulation.
3. Export sales—United States. 4. Foreign trade
regulation—United States. I. Gilbert, Ralph J.
II. Title.
K1030.4.H34 1985 343'.0878 85-560
ISBN 0-03-001679-7 (alk. paper) 342.03878

Published in 1985 by Praeger Publishers
CBS Educational and Professional Publishing
a Division of CBS Inc.
521 Fifth Avenue, New York, NY 10175 USA

56789 052 987654321

Printed in the United States of America
on acid-free paper

ACKNOWLEDGMENTS

A special thanks to Ralph Gilbert, my co-author, for his guidance in choice of subject matter and for his consistent cooperation in moving things along when I seemed to bog down periodically. A special nod should go, finally, to my wife, Patricia, who gracefully endured the usual editorial frustrations as well as gently pushed me forward to complete this work.

R. Duane Hall, Ph.D.
Scottsdale, Arizona
November 1984

In preparing Chapters 3 through 6 of this volume, I have relied heavily on contributions from my partners Michael Coleman (European Common Market agency and distributor appointments), Thomas Johnson (U.S. Export Trading Company Act of 1982), and John McKenzie (U.S. Export Controls and Anti-boycott Regulations). I also am deeply indebted to my partners Neal Block and Robert Gareis for their perceptions and insights, nurtured by our frequent arguments and debate, on the Foreign Corrupt Practices Act, the Domestic International Sales Corporation, and the Foreign Sales Corporation. These and many other of my colleagues have added immeasurably to whatever strengths this book has. My secretary, Miss Marilyn Elliott, deserves a special medal for extraordinary care and cheerfulness in placing the manuscript in final form for the publisher. Finally, I wish to thank my co-author, Dr. Duane Hall, without whose inspiration and prodding this project would not have been undertaken.

Ralph Gilbert
Chicago, Illinois
November 1984

CONTENTS

MULTINATIONAL DISTRIBUTION

1

MARKETING ABROAD

OBJECTIVES

Prior to the 1960s only a small percentage of U.S.-produced goods were exported, while an equally small percentage of foreign-made goods entered the U.S. marketplace. In 20 years the situation has changed dramatically. Today 70 percent of U.S.-made goods are actively competing with foreign-made goods in U.S. markets.[1] Many U.S. producers, sensibly, have opted to meet foreign competition head on in foreign markets rather than attempt merely to maintain their market share in an increasingly competitive U.S. market. Thus, a cardinal corporate growth objective frequently is to augment international sales. This growth must generate enough profits to support the company's cost of capital. Cash flow rates of return on additional working capital, fixed assets, or equity investments should be expected to continue above the company average over the longer term. More often than not these objectives can be met, because export profit margins for a company tend to be higher, and export profits are more lightly taxed than domestic profits (see Chapter 6).

In meeting its export growth objective, a company should have a policy that divisions and other units do not give up options and legal rights to all world markets through long-term exclusive contracts, licensing, surrender of equity or management control, or by other means, without considering long-term alternatives and securing approval at senior corporate levels.

Charters and Responsibilities

Corporate units can have worldwide marketing responsibility for their product lines and should determine, with group management, the most effective worldwide organization for their operations, including considerations of working through company marketing organizations.

Senior management should review all proposals and seek opportunities to combine efforts with all units to provide the greatest overall profit potential.

Corporate staff departments and regional offices should have responsibility in their functional areas and, as well, provide assistance and support to line management to help reach profit and strategic growth objectives of each business unit.

Key Factors for Success

The following key factors are critical in developing a successful export program.

Products

A product must not only fit market needs but be tested thoroughly for reliability in its home market to be successful internationally. A minimum of one year of production testing of all new models should be a guideline. A strong market position at "home" is also important because customers will be greatly influenced by the market position of each product in its country of origin.

Target Markets

There is a critical need to expand knowledge of markets, including market size and growth and thorough evaluation of competitive strength. The most attractive markets, short and long term, should be "targets," with the number limited to a unit's capability. Satisfactory profit is dependent upon achieving a leading market position which is possible only with full support of all functional areas. To be most successful, an exporter must generally have a high percentage of repeat business from satisfied customers. Profit potential is diminished when a high proportion of business is with new customers, since start-up sales, service, and training of customer personnel add to costs.

Organization

Guidelines for structuring a global enterprise are displayed in Exhibit 1.1.

Exhibit 1.1 Guidelines for Structuring the Global Enterprise

1. Establish the shortest practical line of communication between the customer and a company's product and technical support sources.
2. Establish effective sales coverage of headquarter offices of multi-national customers where headquarters is involved in purchasing products for international applications.
3. Seek group and corporate marketing support for major corporations which are regularly contacted by others in a company.
4. Provide sales representation, with area knowledge and language capability, as close to the customer as practical.
5. Where purchasing decisions are made at a political level, establish and maintain contacts with decision-makers (including embassies) in both Washington and the capital of the country involved.
6. Maintain effective communication within the company. One or more units often have key contacts and an established market position. This may often pave the way for sale of other products.

Personnel

Acceleration of international development will require more high-quality personnel skilled in the intricacies of the company, and managing an export business requires added depth in many functions.

Financing

Since financing is often a key factor in sales, competitive financing must be available. Financing is an ongoing company program.

Turnkey Projects/Sales Packages

In some product areas, substantial opportunities are available by putting together complete turnkey projects or a sales package including installation, start-up, and after-sales service. This may involve using products from several units, plus outside technology and products. This capability is critical in developing countries.

Pricing and Sourcing

Prices must be competitive, but a resourceful and flexible marketing package and well-developed personal relationships will avoid the need to have the lowest prices. Market knowledge and up-to-date information on competitive pricing is critical in determining whether or not more than one product source may be necessary.

Currency exchange rates fluctuate widely at times, which affect competitive pricing and sourcing decisions. Personnel responsible for these functions must keep current not only on day-to-day changes but on trends.

Metrication

Major attention must be given to metrication for products which are manufactured in more than one country and which have a substantial world market. Other products can be given lower priority and metrication may be necessary only in sales and service catalogs. Continuing pressure will occur to furnish additional equipment to metric specifications.

Front-End Investment/Control

A successful export program requires strong continuing interest and commitment by all management. The large U.S. market is easier to handle and, too often, exports are "welcomed" during slow periods but neglected when the U.S. economy is strong. This situation must be avoided; the export business must receive consistent high priority.

A substantial early investment in manpower may be required. This investment should be a part of the marketing plan for each target country, and accounting records should be established to track actual expenditures and results against the plan. Careful tracking will result in changing emphasis when market conditions change.

Target-Country Marketing Plans

Each unit should prepare a series of target-country marketing plans for countries in which chances for success are greatest. These plans will then become a part of long-range plans. The exporter should develop profiles of selected countries for reference, to include political and social data as well as economic projections and trends on trade and bank borrowing, balance of payments, and gross national product.

Unit personnel must maintain extensive direct contact with target-country markets. Product specialists must have good product knowledge of competition. The international department should issue specific instructions on writing, reviewing, and monitoring target-country marketing plans.

Export Sales

Export sales comprise any sale of product or technology outside the country where the product is manufactured or the technology is based.

A sales contract may be originated by the "source" unit or by another unit if it has marketing responsibility in the country of sale. Interdivision sales can be cleared through internal sales accounts.

Top priority should be given to export sales from source countries. Managements should source so as to maximize long-term profit growth and still meet acceptable financial criteria. Close coordination and control is required to avoid conflicting and competing quotations from more than one source.

Many developing or "Third World" countries have similar market characteristics. Business is usually controlled by a small, close-knit, and powerful elite. Purchasing decisions are often made by a few individuals either in or strongly influenced by government. Buyers' decisions are often based upon confidence in both the individual they are dealing with and the individual's organization rather than product feature or price.

Success in such countries depends heavily on perception of the credibility of a company, strengthened by a corporate presence appropriate to the market. Prompt response and continual communication are critical in building and maintaining overall credibility.

Export Supporting Equity Investments

Foreign investment is a strategic decision. It may cause exposure to political or economic turmoil, with exchange rate fluctuations and other risks for which there is little protection or control. It requires an understanding of both the culture of the country and its economy.

Corporate management should recognize that pure exporting from the United States over the long term cannot be expected to continue. To achieve a high percentage of world market opportunities, a company must support off-shore sourcing for export. No long-range plan is complete without considering these possibilities.

Investment may not require the construction of major facilities or acquisitions. A start can be made with independent contract manufacturers and small assembly operations.

For foreign joint-venture equity investments, a major objective should be to gain majority or management control immediately, thus creating a "captive" export customer. However, certain conditions may warrant gaining this control over a reasonable length of time, rather than immediately. Minority positions are required by law in some countries, and sometimes may even be desirable, but management control is the key to long-term success. Without it, an exporter must rely upon long-term contractual purchase commitments by the foreign joint-venture company.

Licensing

Licensing (i.e., the export of technology) is generally the least desirable means of getting into a market. A frequent side effect is that the U.S. licensor creates an entrenched competitor abroad. There may be opportunities, however, when no other means of market access is available, when risks of investment cannot be justified, or when the product is nearing the end of its life cycle in its current market. In the computer field, e.g., where product life may be on the order of 18 to 36 months, and the exporter may be "production bound," an aggressive license program with stiff up-front disclosure fees, per unit royalties, and guaranteed minima can yield attractive returns which, otherwise, would be forfeited.

Outside Sales Representatives

Where the product or service for export is highly specialized in a focused market, a direct presence by the exporter may be the only viable approach. Only the exporter's own personnel are sufficiently skilled and fully committed to the product to ensure market credibility and penetration. In most cases, however, it is desirable to engage a local agent or distributor who has customer contacts and market knowledge and can provide both sales and service. A thorough screening of all new representatives and a continuing program of support and evaluation of existing representatives are essential.

When a change or new representative is involved, the operating unit should contact the international department, explain the need, and seek names of candidates from corporate files. The exporter's legal exposure also should be determined before appointing or terminating a foreign representative.

An exporter should contact others who are active in the area and benefit from their experiences and information. The company then should interview all candidates and obtain the following information in writing: (1) Primary business of candidate, outlining characteristics of greatest benefit. Identify owners, officers, key personnel, office and service centers with address, telephone, and telex numbers. (2) Annual sales volume for past three years, company names, and products or other lines handled. (3) End-market and primary customers served. (4) Product specialization and geography served. (5) Spare parts and technical service capability. (6) Business and credit references.

If the above information obtained appears favorable, the exporter should contact the U.S. Department of Commerce representatives or Commercial Attache in the country to verify company reputation and to get any recommendations on other candidates. See Chapter 2 for further discussion of locating and evaluating foreign representatives.

Regional Offices

Regional offices can be established to further sales in a geographical area by recognizing and identifying opportunities and by providing regional business expertise to corporate, group, and other management.

The primary duties of a regional office are to carry out company policies and objectives in the region by presenting its total capabilities and strengths to major customers. This effort requires good communications and teamwork and a thorough understanding that each unit, by its own good performance, can help all others and that total company success will, in turn, benefit each unit. It is important to develop high-level government and commercial contacts to acquaint them with company capabilities and to uncover specific business opportunities.

A regional office can assist in analyzing marketing, acquisition, joint-venture, licensing, and purchasing opportunities, as well as follow through, as appropriate. Furthermore, it can assist in selecting, assigning, and supervising regional personnel, as requested. Other benefits are assistance in selecting and supervising sales agents, as requested, or in providing trip planning, appointments, and local marketing advice to visiting personnel. The offices collectively provide a common denominator among various activities in all regions and can handle special regional business problems within all levels of management.

Regional managers can communicate directly, as appropriate, with all corporate staffs. Business units are responsible for searching out business, quotations, pricing, and closing orders but could also work closely with regional managers on selecting agents, high-level contacts, contract terms, financing, warranty problems, etc., where regional "know-how" and contacts are beneficial or a consistent posture is desirable.

Sales and Services Offices

An exporter planning to set up a sales or service office overseas should work with the international department in coordinating legal and tax considerations. It may also be possible to combine requirements of other departments to reduce costs, improve communications, and strengthen the company's image.

Corporate Business Advisors

Consultants or business advisors may be used in areas to assist in establishing contacts and helping to develop business opportunities. Recommendations for such assistance should come from operating units, although a consultant may be retained and controlled by the international department.

Not all exporters earn the same return. Some advantageous generic strategies to be considered could be:

1. Be the innovator—develop products at the leading edge.
2. Be a fast follower—price, capacity addition.
3. Shared experience—leverage skills from somewhere else—enter late, but have strong transfer skills.
4. Segmented focus—target selected marketplace.
5. Preempt change—identify *early* changes or trends and capitalize on them.
6. Hope! Try to survive under industry leaders.

COMPETITION

The "matrix idea" is a useful marketing tool which should be used in research or planning. Basically it is a way to position products, companies, etc., into a matrix with known, published, or easy-to-obtain facts. Matrices offer these advantages: (1) easy visualization of market position; (2) a simple way to assemble and compare data; (3) knowledge of where you really are in the scheme of things.

A fundamental matrix is the product/price matrix, which permits an exporter to position a product or model against other similar products in terms of a common denominator. A complex matrix can be devised using a company, product line, or product and adding prices, costs, end-use segments, channels of distribution, growth rates, and other factors.

Table 1.1 Sample Matrix

		Major Competitors		
Factors	YOU	A	B	C
Market share	16%	29%	12%	10%
Share trend	Up	Down	Down	Steady
Price	Medium	Low	Medium	High
Customer service	High	Medium	Low	Low
Value Package	High	Medium	Low	Medium
Sales strength	High	Medium	Low	High
Promotional Strength	Low	High	Low	Medium
Marketing mode	Build	Hold	Harvest	Hold
Investment resources	High	Low	Low	Medium

A marketing strength matrix defines what the competitors are bringing to bear against you and where your opportunities and threats lie.

A useful and flexible matrix in which an exporter can employ a wide range of factors to help reveal the competitive pressures against it and the opportunities (weaknesses of your competitors) that can be exploited to gain or hold market share is shown in Table 1.1.

Other factors that could be employed in such a matrix are: product mix, technology, product development, profitability, costs, response time, market "hold," customer benefits, and product features.

PRICING

There are various types of pricing to be considered in establishing a distribution pricing policy overseas. One approach is the "target return," or determination of return on investment margins. This becomes a variable strategy where there is no established competitive product or where high product differentiation will permit a higher price.

A second approach is demand pricing. This is found frequently in commodities. The price is plotted at a point on a demand curve to produce target volume and profitability.

Investment pricing is an approach to deliberately set a low price to build market share against competition or, in a new product field, to build demand more rapidly. It could be risky in an established repetitive product market because the concept invites retaliation by the low-cost high-market-share competitor. Another alternative is exploitative pricing. Here a high price is set to take advantage of exclusivity in a product or an extremely high product differentiation.

Risk pricing takes into consideration the risks involved in the engineering, installation, and start-up of highly customized products and systems. These risks are then considered factors in the product costing. In the "razor blade" approach, the idea is deliberate low pricing of the "razor" to stimulate blade sales, i.e., wear parts, expendables, etc., after-market sales, add-on sales, or services.

Other pricing wrinkles include shop-load pricing, which deliberately sets prices to maintain shop loading during a low-order period. Another tactic is negative pricing. Here a high price is established to discourage orders for a specific product, or for a period when the shop is overloaded. Balanced competitive pricing, also called trade-off pricing, takes into consideration the going rate, differentiation and value package, business center margin needs, and all other factors that may impact the company, customer base, and competition. Finally, flexible pricing can be used as a dynamic and aggressive element of total strategy to build market share or to capture desired orders.

The ultimate pricing strategy will be integrated into the marketing mix directed to identified target market segment, by country, and should be discussed thoroughly with any potential agents, distributors, or brokers.

CUTTING COSTS AND TIME IN MARKETING RESEARCH

What does an exporter really need to know? This is the first question to ask if you want to get the most out of a lean research budget. Research that pays off is not necessarily spelled s-u-r-v-e-y, and does not necessarily require direct consumer interviewing or a fat well-documented report.

More often than not, a handful of reasonably hard facts is enough to make your marketing effort more productive. Shortcut methods can also pay off with much vital detail.

Two real-life examples are: (1) One stubborn market entry problem could have required surveying a large and expensive sample to define the real volume markets; the needed information was developed in just four days. (2) For a consumer product, it might have taken thousands of dollars to develop full market information; the shortcut purchase price was under $400 for a total picture of a national market.

Shortcut research methods are for managers willing to settle for what they need to know. The best place to start is by defining what you know about your markets; then note the information gaps that *must* be filled. This exercise may purge your mind of all the things it might be nice to know, and place the focus on essentials. Shortcut methods may fail to provide thick reports, a wealth of charts and tables, and all the sophistication and certainty of a completely documented survey, but it is not hard to live with what shortcut methods may offer in exchange. They can sharply reduce costs and time, and often they can provide the basic facts upon which good marketing decisions can be made.

POLITICS

Some basic political questions to be answered upon entering a country for the first time are:

1. What is the political structure of the country?
2. Under what type of economic system does the country operate?
3. Is my industry in the public or private sector?
4. It it is in the public sector, does the government also allow private competition in that sector?

Exhibit 1.2 Domestic versus International Planning

Domestic Planning	International Planning
1. Single language and nationality	1. Multilingual/multinational/multicultural factors
2. Relatively homogeneous market	2. Fragmented and diverse markets
3. Data available, usually accurate, and collection easy	3. Data collection a formidable task, requiring significantly higher budgets and personnel
4. Political factors relatively unimportant	4. Political factors frequently vital
5. Relative freedom from government interference	5. Involvement in national economic plans; government influences business decisions
6. Individual corporation has little effect on environment	6. "Gravitational" distortion by large companies
7. Chauvinism helps	7. Chauvinism hinders
8. Relatively stable business environment	8. Multiple environments, many of which are highly unstable (but may be highly profitable)
9. Uniform financial climate	9. Variety of financial climates ranging from over-conservative to wildly inflationary
10. Single currency	10. Currencies differing in stability and real value
11. Business "rules of the game" mature and understood	11. Rules diverse, changeable and unclear
12. Management generally accustomed to sharing responsibilities and using financial controls	12. Management frequently autonomous and unfamiliar with budgets and control

Source: William W. Cain, "International Marketing: Mission Impossible?" *Columbia Journal of World Business* (July-August 1976): 58.

5. If it is in the private sector, is there any tendency to move it toward public ownership?
6. Does the government view foreign capital as being in competition or in partnership with public or local private enterprise?
7. In what ways does the government control the nature and extent of private enterprise?
8. How much of a contribution is the private sector expected to make in helping the government formulate overall economic objectives?

The above points will guide an exporter on the political vulnerability of a given product policy.

PRODUCT STANDARDIZATION

Some choices will have to be made to adapt the physical product to overseas markets. Some factors encourage standardized products internationally, such as economies of scale in production, economies in product research and development, economies in marketing, consumer mobility, the U.S. image, the impact of technology, and operating via exports. Other factors favor product adaptation, such as differing use conditions, other market factors, the influence of government, and company history and operations.

In some situations, simple extension of both product configuration and communications platform will suffice. Once the product-mix considerations are resolved, attention can be channeled toward setting policies and mechanisms to effectively manage the network as established abroad. Planning operations and selling policies can be painfully different as illustrated in Exhibit 1.2. Once the contrasts are identified and understood, one can proceed more confidently to setting up the distribution network.

NOTE

1. Robert Reich, *The Next American Frontier* (New York: Times Books, 1983), p. 121.

2

SETTING UP THE NETWORK

Is there a market? If not, what does an exporter need to do to create one? Creating a need from scratch requires a major effort including the following steps: (1) selling the concept; (2) educating the market; (3) promoting the product.

In most cases, a market does exist, but how large is it? Statistics are usually scarce but available. As to the customers, one needs to discover their buying patterns. Another major concern is identifying the competitors. The net result should be a sales plan covering a period of two to five years.

Inevitably, there are some constraints; some examples include financial considerations such as taxes (inventories, sales), duties, and collections and/or credit procedures. Others include the technical side, such as the issues of how your product meets local requirements: (1) 220 V-50 HZ; (2) standards; (3) local content requirements; (4) unusual inspections. How costly are the necessary modifications?

Turning to the political side, what part of the market is "protected" and how is protection achieved? What about legal constraints, such as import requirements or export documentation?

Marketing overseas is like marketing at home with the right product, proper resources, and a methodology; but, in addition, it requires a thorough understanding of the markets and the local laws and constraints. Finally, marketing overseas takes determination.

THE DISTRIBUTOR

A distributor is a resident representative who promotes and services an exporter's product in a designated "primary" territory. The distributor takes title to the goods, inventories them, and fills orders from the stock, and may also service the product, maintain a supply of spare parts, and conduct local promotion.

There are two basic kinds of distributors: (1) general-line distributors who carry a broad range of products; (2) specialist distributors who usually handle a narrow line of related products.

In the case of both industrial and consumer goods, marketing research is the main responsibility of the principal or manufacturer. Advertising, trade-fair work, and sales promotion usually become joint responsibilities. The chief responsibility of a distributor is sales/service/administration. In other words, the distributor provides the personal contact which transforms overall marketing efforts into sales. The distributor prevents present customers from becoming ex-customers by servicing what is sold, and makes the product available in quantities the customer wants, at locations which permit prompt delivery.

Advantages of Distributors

There are many factors which dictate marketing overseas through a distributor. A good distributor will have an in-place sales network, and perhaps several branch offices to cover his territory adequately, and likely will have an inside track concerning methods of importation, business practices, and methods of selling a particular territory. The distributor's knowledge can save both time and money for an exporter. The distributor would know where the exporter's target market segments would be, and would also know which forms of media would be most effective. Selling to a distributor may help reduce the credit risks which would be involved in selling directly to many customers. Implicit in this statement is the reduced cost of credit-rating investigations.

Acquiring a distributor is probably one of the easiest and least costly ways of entering foreign markets. Such distributors are an effective local medium for obtaining credit information, industry leads, or opening doors for government business. If a country feels hostile toward U.S. subsidiaries or makes it difficult to establish a subsidiary, a distributor provides a means to help avoid such antagonism. In other words, a distributor keeps a market accessible.

Disadvantages of Distributors

The following are some of the disadvantages of using distributors. (See, also, Exhibit 2.1.) Some allege that distributors often cause exporters

Exhibit 2.1 Conflicting Points of View

Exporter	Distributor
Nonexclusive for territory	Exclusive for territory
Minimum territory	Large territory
Exclusive for product	Nonexclusive for products
Short-term contract	Long-term contract
Annual sales quota	No quota—best effort
Price increase option	Price protection
Inventory commitment	Delivery commitment
Scheduled delivery	On demand
Market feedback	Product information
Cost pricing	Market pricing
Unconditional termination	Financial compensation on termination

headaches regarding stocking and servicing inadequacies. When this occurs, the exporter may suffer loss of sales. Customers who cannot get what they want or be serviced properly will naturally look elsewhere. Unless a manufacturer has a company representative overseas working relatively closely with a distributor, control may become difficult.

It is often a challenge to motivate a distributor to make a strong promotion and selling effort for the exporter's product. This is especially common with general-line distributors who handle many product lines and divide their time and efforts too broadly. Usually a foreign distributor receives a fractionally higher profit (trade discount) than a domestic distributor may receive, due to the import documentation and procedural red tape required of the distributor, plus the fact that it is necessary to deal with a longer supply pipeline. This longer pipeline means that the distributor has more capital tied up, thus a "sweetener" is almost a must. Finally, in many countries it is difficult to terminate a distributor's contract without incurring high costs and/or penalties.

Tasks

A distributor performs a variety of tasks; the more prominent ones are:

1. Taking title to the product
2. Stocks
3. Selling locally and promoting the products/services
4. Carrying inventories
5. Extending credit to customers

Manufacturers must support their distributor networks via financial assistance in promotion programs, training of distributor personnel, technical and delivery support, and acceptable credit arrangements. In selection, pick those who are established with good contacts. Lines should be complementary. Other important points are: financial stability, technical competence, and a willingness to assign personnel to your product lines on a full-time basis. Obtaining good people is the key.

Responsibilities of a Distributor to an Exporter

In negotiations with a distributor an exporter should stress the following points:

1. Maximization of sales of manufacturer's products.
2. Prompt payment within the terms of the agreement.
3. Taking full advantage of manufacturer's expertise, resources, and knowledge.
4. Providing full cooperation during manufacturer's in-field visits.
5. Regular communication with the manufacturer in the form of sales reports, requests for supportive resources, information of sales successes and failures.
6. Aggressive promotion throughout the territory.
7. Operation in accordance with good business standards.
8. Development of a good business reputation locally.
9. Being sales minded as well as profit minded.
10. Maintenance of regular product inventory control.

Responsibilities of an Exporter to a Distributor

On the other hand, an exporter should not forget its obligation to the distributor:

1. Education of the distributor.
2. Establishment of sales goals.
3. Compensation arrangements.
4. Credit terms agreed upon.
5. Development of identified distributor personnel.

6. Development of identified distributor personnel.
7. Guarantees.
8. Agreements.
9. Reporting assignments.

Checking Things Out

Many pitfalls can be avoided if an exporter does a thorough job of investigating a distributor or agent before *any* agreement is drawn up.

An investigation begins with obtaining names of potential representation in overseas markets. For this there are several sources. Knowledge of these sources definitely facilitates the process of locating someone who fulfills the exporter's expectations. Many sources should be utilized.

One source is U.S. manufacturers of related types of products. Checking with a U.S. manufacturer who exports related but noncompeting products through distributors or agents is beneficial to the exporter, for he may be able to locate a good sales network already in operation. Advertising in international trade publications can be helpful in locating names of possible representatives.

The U.S. Department of Commerce offers an Agents and Distributor Search Program as a special service to help find intermediaries. For a nominal fee and a short wait, the exporter can receive a report which lists several recommendations. Do not forget U.S. trade centers and commercial fairs. These offer the U.S. manufacturer a good opportunity to interview local distributors and agents and to exhibit products overseas. U.S. trade missions are selected groups of businessmen who carry specific U.S. business proposals to certain foreign markets. If a manufacturer wishes to locate intermediaries in a certain market, he can submit his proposal to the trade mission well in advance of its scheduled departure.

Direct mail is always an option. In this case, the U.S. manufacturer could obtain a trade list from the U.S. Chamber of Commerce, showing the names and addresses of foreign distributors or agents grouped by country and by industry or services. Furthermore, trade development departments of many commercial banks, steamship lines, airlines, port authorities, and marine insurance companies have active trade development departments. Since the manufacturer may be a potential customer, these entities often help by suggesting possible outlets.

Selecting a Distributor

First, a manufacturer should conduct a thorough self-appraisal, since there are many questions a potential exporter has to answer before selecting a distributor. These answers are important, for they invariably influence selection. The following should be seriously considered:

1. What is the company's distribution philosophy? Does the company want exclusive or nonexclusive distribution? Would an intensive distribution philosophy, which establishes widespread distribution through multiple distributors, be best?

2. What can the manufacturer offer to ensure cooperation (i.e., credit policies, wholesale margins, advertising support, training for sales and service personnal, market research support)?

3. What type of control devices does the manufacturer wish to have (i.e., service requirements, advertising and promotion minima)?

After such soul searching is accomplished, a manufacturer is prepared to check his list of prospective distributors to obtain information on the products the party presently sells, names and addresses of all companies represented, and the number of salespersons on the staff.

Other questions concern the number of branch offices and where they are located, a list of bank and trade references, the exact territory in which salespersons make calls, and the names of the officials in the company.

Inquire when the company was founded, and whether or not the distributor or agent has had experience selling products similar to the manufacturer's products. Check out the services offered and the sales policy. Is the organization progressive or conservative? Does the firm advertise?

Observe the location. Are transportation facilities adequate in his location to cover the territory? Ascertain the political influence of the intermediary. If the government is to be an important customer, having political influence could be important.

Normally, an exporter will not receive all of this information; however, it should strive to obtain as much data as possible to be able to narrow down the number of prospective appointees.

The exporter should commence a thorough credit check. This credit investigation can give the exporter a feel for the company's reputation, credit ranking, and a record of payment. Mercantile agency reports, such as Dun and Bradstreet, furnish overseas credit reports for a nominal fee. World Trade and Data Reports' from the U.S. Department of Commerce give information about the performance record of a firm, trading experience, a listing of lines handled, capitalization, and annual turnover. Also, credit and sales information may be obtained by asking other U.S. suppliers who are selling to these same parties.

At this point an exporter should begin to feel relatively comfortable with the data. Next, it should go overseas for a final check.

Later On

Basically, a close coordination between the exporter and the distributor is required to increase the probability that the export program will be effective. Probably the best way to control a distributor's activities is with a liaison person. This liaison should have authority to make "on-the-spot" decisions. Having this authority definitely benefits the distributor, since it eliminates the need for continual contact with the exporter's head office. There are other important functions which a liaison can perform. He can work with the distributor in increasing sales and solving local market problems. The liaison person should make regular visits, but not so frequently that the distributor feels as if he is being spied upon. Finally, a liaison person should be able to supply the exporter answers to these following questions:

1. How are the distributor's actual sales measuring up against planned targets?
2. How do his sales compare with past performance?
3. Is the product displayed effectively?
4. How does the exporter compare with competition?
5. How much time does the distributor spend on the exporter's product lines compared to other lines?
6. How does the distributor divide his sales force; which part of the force sells the exporter's product?
7. If the distributor has a showroom, how much space is afforded to the exporter's product line?

Another form of control is to set up sales quotas. The quota should be mutually agreed upon. A quota system often works well when an incentive (i.e., a trip, a bonus) is attached to it.

Control also materializes through reports. The reports usually consist of information on sales (broken down by product and type of sale), levels of inventory, activity on after-sales servicing, competitive activity, and new products in the market. Most companies require reports at least quarterly. Control fosters efficiency, effectiveness, and peace of mind.

THE AGENT

An agent is a resident representative who promotes the sale of an exporter's product to customers in a designated territory. An agent is, in effect, a foreign instrument of the exporter (rather than an independent businessman), earning a commission on sales of the exporter's products in the agent's appointed territory. An agent normally takes no business or credit risks, as does a distributor. Chapter 4 expands upon this distinction between a distributor and an agent. All of the considerations in locating, screening, appointing, and terminating distributors apply with equal force to agents.

Should an Exporter Terminate?

Why terminate? There are a variety of possible reasons:

1. To establish a direct marketing entity or manufacturing/assembly operation.
2. To replace an existing distributor/agent.
   a. "Poor" performance.
   b. Only "adequate" performance.
   c. Replace distributor/agent of an acquired company with your own marketing office or your own distributor/agent.
   d. Replace distributor with agent or vice versa.
3. To move out of the market.
   a. Insufficient volume to support expense.
   b. Political reasons: change of government; exchange controls; closure of border.

A series of checklists to help in establishing appointees is reflected in Exhibits 2.2-2.8. While not inclusive, lists permit an orderly approach to the selection and management process in overseas markets.

Exhibit 2.2 Planning Checklist

- Distribution channels
  - Rep
  - Agent
  - Distributor

(Exhibit 2.2 continues)

Exhibit 2.2 continued

- • Subsidiary
- • Licensee
- Market knowledge/performance
- Pricing
  - • Discounts
  - • Commissions
- Financial terms
  - • L/C
  - • Open account
  - • Terms
- Technical competence required
  - • Engineering back-up
  - • Service
- Partnership approach

Exhibit 2.3 General Sources of Information

I. Domestic Initiative (U.S. Department of Commerce)
  A. Trade opportunity program.
  B. Catalog exhibitions.
  C. Foreign buyer program.
  D. New product information service.
  E. Foreign market reports service (NTIS).
  F. Commerce today.
  G. Overseas product sales and major export projects.
  H. A.I.D. procurement information bulletin.
II. Overseas Initiative (U.S. Department of Commerce)
  A. U.S. trade centers, U.S. trade fairs abroad (overseas export promotion calendar).
  B. Trade announcements service.
  C. Between-show promotions (trade centers).
  D. Trade missions.
  E. In-store promotions (consumer goods only).

Exhibit 2.4 Identifying Representation Candidates

I. Government Sources
  A. U.S. Department of Commerce programs.
    1. Export mailing list; data tape service.

(Exhibit 2.4 continues)

Exhibit 2.4 continued

      2. Trade lists.
          a. Business firms and state trading organizations.
          b. Global market survey, trade lists.
      3. Agent/distributor service.
      4. U.S. trade centers.
   B. State agencies overseas.
   C. U.S. embassies and consulates.
   D. Foreign embassies and consulates in U.S.

II. Institutional Contacts
   A. Banks.
      1. Your commercial bank.
      2. Foreign resident banks.
   B. Attorneys.
   C. Advertising agencies.
   D. Accounting firms.

III. Private Trade Lists.
   A. Dunn and Bradstreet.
   B. Blytmann International, P.O. Box 10700, Bainbridge, WA 98110.
   C. Local phone books.
   D. "American Firms, Subsidiaries and Affiliates Operating in Foreign Countries" (World Trade Academy Press, 50 East 42 St., New York, NY 10017).

IV. Transportation Industry
   A. Foreign forwarders.
   B. Airlines.
   C. Shipping agents.

V. Chambers of Commerce and Trade Associations
   A. Foreign chambers in the United States ("World Yearbook of Chambers of Commerce").
   B. U.S. chambers overseas.
   C. Foreign chambers overseas.
   D. World trade centers association.
   E. "Trade Directories of the World" (Croner Publications, Inc., Queen's Village, NY 11428).

VI. Miscellaneous
   A. Related U.S. exporters doing business in country or region.
   B. Personal/business contacts in country or region.
   C. Mailing lists from magazines or trade associations.

Exhibit 2.5 Selection Process

- Set your objectives/needs
  - Industry sources
  - U.S. Department of Commerce
  - U.S. foreign embassies/consulates
  - In-country search
  - Advertising
- Qualifying mailing and questionnaire
- Check references/credit rating
- Evaluate
- Market trip—interview
- Evaluate and select
- Written agreement
  - Responsibilities
  - Exclusive—noncompetitive
  - Duration
- Develop joint marketing plan
- Ongoing support and evaluation

Exhibit 2.6 Representatives' Data Form

Name of Organization: Date:

Principals: 1   2

Address:
          Street   City   State   Zip

Telephone No.:   (   )
                    Area   Number

1. No. of years in business:

2. Territory covered:

3. Branch locations:

4. No. of salesmen:

5. How many sales calls per month can your
   organization commit to our line?

(Exhibit 2.6 continues)

Exhibit 2.6 continued

  6. Gross sales volume last year: $

  7. Do you have your own advertising/promotion
     program?   Yes   No

  8. Do you have stocking facilities?   Yes   No

  9. Do you have a service staff?   Yes   No

 10. Please list bank references:

11.	Manufacturers currently represented (include addresses)	Products	Territory	No. of years representing
12.	Principal customers		Approximate $ volume sold to each last year	

Exhibit 2.7 Support and Evaluation

- Set performance levels based on set objectives
- In-country support
  - Share of time
- Communication
  - Information sharing
- Promotion
  - Advertising
  - Brochures
  - Audio/visual
  - Trade shows

(Exhibit 2.7 continues)

Exhibit 2.7 continued

- Training
  - Sales
  - Service
  - Technical manuals
- Field training—ongoing
  - Sales meetings
- Stocking
  - Parts
  - Machines
  - Payment terms

Exhibit 2.8 Overseas Trip

"Package" to take on your overseas trip—take enough copies, plus extras.

1. Annual reports—your company and list of bank references.
2. List of present overseas representatives, if any, and short history of each.
3. Selected product literature, depending on product assortment.
4. Sample representative contracts.
5. Price lists (C.I.F.) to each country, for each product.
6. Explanation of sales commissions, terms, etc.—order system explanation.
7. Information on exclusion or nonexclusion and why? Will you provide a contract?
8. Information on support you are willing to provide and actions you seek from representatives.
9. Translation of company fact sheets into appropriate foreign languages.

3

THE AGREEMENT

INTRODUCTION

After a U.S. manufacturer (principal) has identified a prospective foreign representative (distributor or commission agent) and is satisfied with his integrity, financial responsibility, community standing, and competence, the next logical consideration is the contract itself. Initially, in drafting the contract, a careful distinction should be drawn between "distributor" and a "sales representative" or "commission agent."

As discussed in Chapter 4, some protective legal jurisdictions grant special statutory protection to distributors to the exclusion of commission agents (e.g., Belgium), while other jurisdictions grant special statutory protection to commission agents to the exclusion of distributors (e.g., France and Italy). As further discussed in Chapter 4, moreover, distributor appointments are subject to European Common Market antitrust rules, while agency appointments are not. Thus, the identification of the appointee—as either a "distributor" or an "agent"— is frequently crucial.

The term "dealer" in many protective jurisdictions, in the legal sense, can mean either a distributor or an agent, although in the business sense it usually connotes a distributor. In many Middle Eastern jurisdictions, the term "agent" is a legal term broadly encompassing both commission agents and distributors.

If contracts are to be entered into with a number of foreign distributors and commission agents, a U.S. exporter should develop both a standard foreign distributor appointment and a standard commission agency appointment. These agreements should incorporate standard terms regarding the territory covered, the scope of the grant, the appointee's responsibilities and obligations, the U.S. manufacturer's obligations, pricing and delivery, term and termination, and related matters. This approach is helpful both in negotiation and in administering multiple contracts. In negotiations, the contract can be characterized as an expression of company policy, with only minimal changes possible. Administratively, multiple contracts can be managed more easily if each has relatively uniform obligations, pricing terms, grounds for termination, notice of termination, and standard general clauses. Ad hoc arrangements entered into by an officer of the U.S. principal often lead to contract disputes that arise long after the officer has left the company. Unless the company's files are meticulously maintained on a contract-by-contract basis, with all relevant correspondence, the principal is at a distinct disadvantage in dealing with appointees. This risk can be largely eliminated by use of a standard appointment that specifically supplants and supersedes all prior agreements or understandings concerning the subject matter of the standard contract. The structure of both distributor and agency appointments is discussed below.

THE DISTRIBUTOR AGREEMENT

A distributor agreement normally begins with a "definitions" article setting forth and defining the products to be covered by the agreement, the territory in which they are to be resold, the effective date of the agreement, and other terms.

Immediately thereafter comes the "grant" clause under which the U.S. exporter (principal) designates and appoints the distributor as its exclusive or nonexclusive appointee in the territory for distribution of the products, subject to the terms of the agreement, and, preferably, "subject to such policies, rules, instruction as principal may issue from time to time with respect to the promotion and sale of the products."

Succeeding sections cover the distributor's undertakings with respect to the agreement. For easy reference, both the distributor's and the principal's undertakings should be set forth in comprehensive separate articles at the beginning of the agreement rather than scattered throughout the document. A more comprehensive distributor appointment would set forth, by way of example, the following 27 basic obligations of the distributor. The purpose of these clauses is to detail the distributor's obligations concerning training of technicians, servicing of the products, advertising, reporting obligations, minimum inventory requirements, minimum purchases, and related issues. *The distributor undertakes the following*:

1. At all times to keep on its payroll not less than ——— skilled salesmen for the purpose of advising and training customers in using the Products in the Territory. For this purpose, within thirty (30) days after the Effective Date of this Agreement DISTRIBUTOR undertakes to send to the facilities of PRINCIPAL in the United States or the facilities of a subsidiary of PRINCIPAL outside the United States, at PRINCIPAL's option, one or more of DISTRIBUTOR's officers and/or employees for initial training in the sale and use of the Products. DISTRIBUTOR shall bear the salaries and all costs of travel and living expenses of its directors and/or employees, while PRINCIPAL will provide classroom instruction at no charge to DISTRIBUTOR.

2. At all times to keep on its payroll not less than ——— skilled technicians for the purpose of maintaining all contract products and equipment in use in the Territory. At a mutually agreed time DISTRIBUTOR undertakes to send to the facilities of PRINCIPAL in the United States or the facilities of a subsidiary of PRINCIPAL outside the United States, at PRINCIPAL's option, one or more of DISTRIBUTOR's directors and/or employees for initial training in the servicing of the Products. DISTRIBUTOR shall bear the salaries and all costs of travel and living expenses of its officers and/or employees, while PRINCIPAL will provide classroom instruction at no charge to DISTRIBUTOR.

3. At all times to assume full and complete responsibility for the installation and maintenance of the Products located in the Territory.

4. To advertise and promote the Products effectively and to use its best efforts to extend the sale of the Products throughout the Territory. All advertising and promotional copy and all translations thereof shall be subject to prior review and written approval by PRINCIPAL. DISTRIBUTOR shall, thirty (30) days prior to the commencement of each Contract Year, submit a proposed advertising and promotion program and budget for PRINCIPAL's approval.

5. Not to design, manufacture, sell, promote, market, or advertise in the Territory any products that PRINCIPAL considers competitive with the Products or with PRINCIPAL's planned lines of additional products during the period of this Agreement and for one (1) year thereafter, without the prior written consent of PRINCIPAL.

6. Neither directly nor through any third party to seek customers for any of the Products or establish any branch or maintain any depot for the distribution of the Products outside the Territory.

7. To effect or secure (and provide copies thereof to PRINCIPAL) all necessary governmental permits, licenses, and registrations required in connection with the importation and resale of the Products in the Territory.

8. To submit to PRINCIPAL at the end of each calendar quarter adequate reports detailing all relevant information as to the prevailing market situation, the attitudes of customers, and the activities of competitors in the Territory.

9. To submit to PRINCIPAL within fifteen (15) days after the end of each calendar quarter a written account of each month's sales of the Products, as well as a report on DISTRIBUTOR's current inventory, and detailed sales projections of the Products for the next twelve (12) months in order to facilitate PRINCIPAL's production and investment plans for the following year.

10. To submit to principal at the end of each calendar quarter a report containing product performance data, including at least the following information for each model number/serial number: number of failures during period, number of emergency calls during period, number of preventive maintenance calls during period, meter readings at beginning and end of period, and down time.

11. To submit to PRINCIPAL, within sixty (60) days of the close of DISTRIBUTOR's fiscal year, photocopies of DISTRIBUTOR's balance sheet, profit and loss statement, and cash flow for the fiscal year just ended.

12. To give representatives from PRINCIPAL the opportunity to participate in sales meetings and exhibitions in order to enable PRINCIPAL to understand marketing problems within the Territory and give adequate assistance when and where required. DISTRIBUTOR shall give ample advance notice to PRINCIPAL of all sales meetings, promotional events, and trade shows concerning the Products within the Territory.

13. To order and keep a representative selection of PRINCIPAL's up-to-date sales literature, price lists, catalogues, samples, demonstration equipment, and other promotional materials in good condition.

14. To maintain such stock of the Products as is reasonably necessary to enable DISTRIBUTOR to comply with its obligations hereunder.

15. To make minimum purchases of the Products from PRIN-CIPAL as set forth in Schedule ––– hereof. In the event this Agreement is extended for Contract Years not referred to in Schedule –––, PRINCIPAL and DISTRIBUTOR shall agree in advance to further minimum purchase quotas for DISTRIBUTOR during such extension period.

16. To actively follow up every lead supplied by PRINCIPAL.

17. To call on each purchaser of the Products in the Territory during the previous year on approximately the anniversary date of such purchase.

18. Not at any time to divulge any confidential information relating to the Products or to PRINCIPAL's affairs or business or method of carrying on business to any third party.

19. Not to appoint, without the prior written approval of PRINCI-PAL, any subdistributors or sales representatives (other than its employees) in the Territory in connection with the performance of this Agreement. In the event that PRINCIPAL grants such approval, it is understood that such appointment shall be made only in the name and for the account of DISTRIBUTOR and shall be for a term no greater than the term of this Agreement. DISTRIBUTOR shall not grant to the subdistributors and/or sales representatives any rights greater than those that are granted by PRINCIPAL to DISTRIBUTOR under this Agreement. DISTRIBUTOR shall also impose on the subdistributors and/or sales representatives the same obligations as PRINCIPAL has imposed on DISTRIBUTOR under this Agreement for the purpose of protecting the goodwill of PRINCIPAL and the Products. DISTRI-BUTOR shall defend, indemnify, and hold PRINCIPAL harmless against any claim, loss, liability, or expense (including attorneys' fees and court costs) arising out of or based upon any claim made by any of DISTRIBUTOR's subdistributors, sales representatives, or employees against PRINCIPAL.

20. To inform PRINCIPAL of any suggestions for modification, variation, or improvement of the Products, including, but not limited to, designs and specifications for the purpose of meeting specific local requirements.

21. To secure PRINCIPAL's prior approval of any change or intended change of management, key sales personnel, or ownership of DISTRIBUTOR, which shall not be unreasonably withheld.

22. Not to make or authorize, without PRINCIPAL's prior written consent, any reproduction of any part of the Products.

23. To ensure that the Products are sold, resold, and advertised in the form and with the labeling or marking designated by PRINCIPAL and not to alter, remove, or interfere therewith without the prior written consent of PRINCIPAL.

24. To take all steps requested by PRINCIPAL to secure for PRINCIPAL any property rights in connection with the Products (including but not limited to PRINCIPAL's patents, trademarks, and copyrights), to respect such property rights of PRINCIPAL, and comply with all local laws and regulations in respect thereof, and to assist PRINCIPAL in taking any steps necessary to defend such rights. Any reasonable expenses incurred in this regard by DISTRIBUTOR shall be reimbursed by PRINCIPAL.

25. To acknowledge at all times PRINCIPAL's exclusive right, title, and interest in and to the patents and trademarks listed in Schedule ——— hereof, which PRINCIPAL has registered in the United States or the Territory, and will not at any time do or cause to be done any act or thing contesting or in any way impairing or tending to impair any part of such right, title, and interest. In connection with any reference to the trademarks, DISTRIBUTOR shall not in any manner represent that it has any ownership interest in the trademarks or registrations thereof. Whenever DISTRIBUTOR refers to the trademarks in advertising or in any other manner to identify the Products, it shall clearly indicate PRINCIPAL's ownership of the trademarks.

26. To use no trade names, corporate names, or trade styles employing the trademarks without the prior written consent of PRINCIPAL, and any such uses and all uses by DISTRIBUTOR of said trade names, corporate names, or trade style shall cease upon the expiration or termination of this Agreement for any reason.

27. Not at any time to make any promises or representations or give any warranties or guarantees with respect to the Products except such as are contained in PRINCIPAL's sales literature for the Products or as are expressly authorized by PRINCIPAL in writing.

Typically, a principal's undertakings under the agreement are not as extensive as those of a distributor. The principal normally agrees to accept and fill all orders of the distributor and make available such manufacturing information and engineering and technical data as may be necessary for the distributor to sell and service the products. The principal normally agrees to furnish the distributor, without charge, an appropriate supply of sales literature, catalogs, and other promotional materials relating to the products, to assist in distributor training and promotional programs, and to forward to the distributor all sales leads and inquiries from potential customers located in the territory. Typical obligations undertaken by the principal are set forth below. *The principal undertakes the following*:

1. To use its best efforts to fill orders of DISTRIBUTOR for the Products hereunder and to make available all modifications of the Products. No order from DISTRIBUTOR for the Products shall be binding upon PRINCIPAL until accepted by PRINCIPAL in writing; the decision to accept or reject any particular order of DISTRIBUTOR shall be reserved to PRINCIPAL's sole judgment. Notwithstanding the foregoing, PRINCIPAL shall not be liable in any way for any loss occurring to DISTRIBUTOR in the event delivery of the Products is frustrated, delayed, or rendered uneconomical to PRINCIPAL by strikes, riots, lockouts, trade disputes, shortages of raw material or components, acts of restraints of governments, a significant increase in prices of components, or by any other cause beyond the reasonable control of PRINCIPAL.

2. To make available to DISTRIBUTOR after execution of this Agreement such know-how, trade secrets, manufacturing information, marketing and application data (including PRINCIPAL's previous experience relating to accounts receivable), and other proprietary, secret, and confidential information owned by PRINCIPAL that, in the opinion of PRINCIPAL, are necessary for DISTRIBUTOR to sell and service the Products. DISTRIBUTOR shall not make use of such confidential information other than in connection with the sale and/or lease and maintenance of the Products sold by PRINCIPAL under this Agreement and shall under no circumstances disclose such confidential information to any other individual, partnership, association, member of a joint venture, corporation, or any other third party.

3. To furnish DISTRIBUTOR, without charge, an appropriate supply of sales literature, price lists, catalogues, samples, technical manuals, and other promotional materials relating to the Products. The promotional materials shall be furnished in the English language and in the system of measurement used by PRINCIPAL. The above items shall remain the property of PRINCIPAL. DISTRIBUTOR shall not translate any of the documentation furnished by PRINCIPAL without first obtaining the prior written approval of PRINCIPAL, and DISTRIBUTOR shall provide copies of such translation to PRINCIPAL. PRINCIPAL may make reasonable charges if more than a

nominal quantity of these promotional materials is supplied to DISTRIBUTOR.

4. To promote and advertise the Products in the Territory at its expense as PRINCIPAL in its sole discretion deems appropriate.

5. To provide DISTRIBUTOR with photocopies of all PRINCIPAL's advertisements, for appropriate use and placement by DISTRIBUTOR within the Territory.

6. To assist DISTRIBUTOR in service training and other programs intended to enhance DISTRIBUTOR's ability to sell and service the Products. It is understood that DISTRIBUTOR shall bear the salaries of any DISTRIBUTOR personnel during such period of training and all costs and travel and living expenses incurred by such personnel in attending such training.

7. To send to the Territory at the request of DISTRIBUTOR, upon reasonable notice and as available, PRINCIPAL's personnel to enable the DISTRIBUTOR to fulfill its obligations under this Agreement. Fees for this service shall be borne by DISTRIBUTOR at the rate of U.S. $500 per day (including travel time) for each of PRINCIPAL's personnel providing such service. Training shall be in English. In addition, DISTRIBUTOR agrees to pay all transportation and living expenses incurred by each of PRINCIPAL's personnel in connection with such service.

8. To forward to DISTRIBUTOR sales leads and inquiries from customers located within the Territory. DISTRIBUTOR shall promptly follow up such leads and report thereon to PRINCIPAL.

9. To warrant the Products as appropriate.

The agreement should cover the pricing and payment terms for the products. Prices to the distributor normally are those specified in the principal's current catalogs or price lists at the time the principal accepts the distributor's purchase order, subject to an agreed discount set forth in a schedule attached to the agreement. Initially, a distributor should be required to open an irrevocable letter of credit in favor of the principal, confirmed by a U.S. bank. As the relationship matures, however, the principal may grant open-account terms.

Shipments under the agreement should be made on the principal's standard shipping terms and conditions, subject always to the provisions of the agreement, which should prevail in the event of any inconsistency. Normally the principal's obligation to effect shipment is fully discharged upon delivery of the products F.O.B. at the principal's manufacturing facility and/or warehouse. A typical clause to this effect is as follows:

Principal's obligation to effect shipment of the Products shall be fully discharged upon delivery of the Products F.O.B. at the manufacturing or warehousing facility of PRINCIPAL in the United States, or, at the option of PRINCIPAL, at the manufacturing or warehousing facility of a subsidiary of PRINCIPAL outside the United States. Title to and all risk of damage or loss to the Products shall pass to DISTRIBUTOR at the above-specified delivery point, and DISTRIBUTOR shall be solely responsible for all costs (including insurance) relating to the transportation of the Products from that delivery point into the Territory.

For tax reasons, a number of companies pass title abroad at the foreign port of shipment. Under Section 862 of the 1954 Internal Revenue Code (the "Code"), one-half of the principal's income on such product sale is thereby characterized as foreign-source income. By increasing its foreign-source income, a principal effectively can increase its annual foreign tax credit limitation under the following formula set forth in Section 904 of the Code:

$$\frac{\text{Principal's foreign source income}}{\text{Principal's worldwide income}} \times \begin{array}{c}\text{U.S. tax } (46\%)\\ \text{on principal's}\\ \text{worldwide}\\ \text{income}\end{array} = \begin{array}{c}\text{Foreign}\\ \text{tax credit}\\ \text{limitation}\end{array}$$

By increasing the numerator of the limiting fraction, the limitation is increased, permitting a higher permissible credit of foreign income taxes paid against the principal's U.S. tax liability.

The principal normally requires that the distributor may not cancel any orders or return previously delivered products without the principal's written consent, in accordance with the terms specified by the principal.

Next, the principal normally sets forth its standard warranty with respect to the products. The principal should not be bound, however, to make good any defect in the products where (1) the products have been subjected to misuse, neglect, or accidental damage; (2) the products have been modified or repaired without the approval of the principal; or (3) the principal's trademarks have been defaced or removed from the products.

Also, the principal should make no representation or warranty that the products will not infringe the trademarks, trade names, or other industrial property rights of third parties.

After stating the warranty with respect to the products, a principal should seek a contractual undertaking from the distributor that the principal will not be derivatively responsible for claims against the distributor. This normally is accomplished by a clause like the following:

> DISTRIBUTOR shall indemnify PRINCIPAL and hold it harmless from any claims, demands, liabilities, suits, or expenses of any kind arising out of DISTRIBUTOR's business, and these provisions shall survive the expiration or termination of this Agreement for any reason and shall be liberally construed in favor of PRINCIPAL.

Next in the agreement, the parties detail the term of the agreement, the circumstances under which renewal can be effected, and causes for termination. The principal should reserve the right to terminate upon giving written notice to the distributor in any of the following events:

1. Any breach of the agreement by DISTRIBUTOR not cured within thirty (30) days after written notice thereof, including breach of any open-account payment terms that may be negotiated by the parties (timely payments thereunder being of the essence).

2. Insolvency of bankruptcy of DISTRIBUTOR and/or the appointment of a trustee or receiver in bankruptcy for DISTRIBUTOR.

3. Inability or failure of DISTRIBUTOR to make payments under the agreement and any inability or prospective failure of distributor to perform its obligations hereunder.

4. A substantial change of management, personnel, or ownership of DISTRIBUTOR effected without the prior written approval of PRINCIPAL.

5. The enactment of a law, decree, or regulations by a governmental unit within the Territory that would impair or restrict the right of PRINCIPAL to terminate or elect not to renew the agreement.

6. The acquisition of direct or indirect control of DISTRIBUTOR by any person, form, company, or entity that manufactures or markets products competing or likely to compete with the Products.

In the event of termination, the parties customarily provide for a return by the distributor of all sales literature, catalogs, samples, demonstration equipment, and like items, as well as a repurchase by principal of the current salable stock of the products held by the distributor, usually at the distributor's inventory cost less an agreed restocking discount for the principal. If the principal elects not to exercise its repurchase option, the distributor is free to sell its remaining stock of products under the same terms and conditions as set forth in the agreement.

The balance of the distributor agreement should cover standard legal matters, such as:

1. "Assignment"—Neither party may assign its rights under the contract without the approval of the other, subject to an exception for a subsidiary or affiliate of the assigning company.
2. "Waiver"—No waiver of a provision by one party is to be deemed a waiver of any succeeding breach of the same or any other provision of the agreement.
3. "Entire Agreement"—The parties agree that the contract reflects the complete and final understandings of the parties with respect to the appointment and cancels and supersedes any prior understandings or agreements between the parties relating to such appointment.
4. "U.S. Laws and Regulations"—The distributor agrees to abide by U.S. export control laws and regulations, as well as the U.S. Foreign Corrupt Practices Act regarding payments to foreign officials.
5. "Governing Law"—The parties normally adhere to U.S. governing law.
6. "Arbitration"—The parties normally agree to U.S. arbitration conducted under the auspices of the American Arbitration Association or the rules of the International Chamber of Commerce. On occasion, the parties agree to special rules among themselves for the handling of arbitration.

Finally, in schedules attached to the distributor appointment, the principal should identify the products covered by the appointment, minimum purchase quotas established for the distributor, the trademarks and patents of the principal relating to the products in both the United States and the territory, and the distributor's discount on the U.S. principal's price.

THE AGENCY (OR SALES REPRESENTATIVE) AGREEMENT

A commission agent or sales representative involved in the promotion and sale of a U.S. principal's goods has obligations that are fundamentally different from those of a distributor. He generally undertakes fewer risks and obligations than does a distributor. In common with the distributor agreement, an agency agreement normally begins with a grant clause under which the agent is appointed as the U.S. principal's exclusive (or nonexclusive) agent in a defined territory for the import, sale, and promotion of agreed products, "subject to all the terms and conditions of principal's corporate policies as they may then or hereafter exist."

Thereafter, the agent's sales activities in promoting firm orders from purchasers from within the territory, for direct sale by the principal to such purchasers, are set out in a list of duties and obligations of the agent as shown below:

1. AGENT shall undertake at his own expense appropriate promotional efforts to achieve a proper recognition of the Products in the Territory.

2. All orders shall be solicited and obtained by AGENT at prices and in accordance with terms and conditions specified by PRINCIPAL. All such prices and terms shall be subject to change on 60 days' notice to AGENT.

3. AGENT shall have no authority to accept orders on behalf of PRINCIPAL or to commit PRINCIPAL to the sale or delivery of any Products, and all solicitations of orders shall be made with the understanding that such orders are subject to acceptance by PRINCIPAL.

4. AGENT shall make only such representations as to quality, capacity, expected life or duration, and similar representations with respect to the Products on which orders may be solicited as may be authorized in writing by PRINCIPAL from time to time.

5. AGENT shall in the first contract year promote firm orders for direct sales of Products by PRINCIPAL to purchasers within the Territory having an aggregate net F.O.B. plant value of U.S. $_____.

6. Except as otherwise specified herein, AGENT shall undertake and continue the performance of this Agreement solely with the employees and facilities presently owned, leased, employed, or contracted by him, and shall not make any investments in fixed assets or otherwise or contract additional employees or agents without the prior written consent of PRINCIPAL, which shall not be unreasonably withheld.

7. AGENT shall refrain from promoting, selling, or offering for sale during the life of this Agreement any goods or articles that in PRINCIPAL's opinion compete with the Products, either directly or indirectly, through an entity that is in any way financially or contractually related to agent.

In addition to the above-outlined activities, the agent also undertakes to furnish the principal with monthly or quarterly operations reports outlining in detail the agent's activities in the territory on behalf of the U.S. manufacturer.

With respect to the agent's right to commissions, the principal, first, should retain an unqualified right, without liability to the agent, to accept, reject, or cancel any such orders received, to modify the contract after the order is accepted, to accept returns, and to determine the time, manner, or sequence of filling orders for any reason whatsoever. Second, a principal normally stipulates that no commission shall accrue to the agent until the full purchase price is received by the principal. Third, a principal normally requires that no commission or payment shall be due the agent for repair and rework services on the products or for engineering services or other special services ordered by customers and performed by the principal's service department.

In a typical appointment, the legal relationship between the parties is carefully defined as follows:

> AGENT agrees that in all matters relating to this agreement he shall be acting as an independent contractor. He shall not have any authority to assume or create any obligations, express or implied, on behalf of PRINCIPAL in any capacity other than as hereinbefore set forth. Nothing in this Agreement shall be construed to give AGENT the right or authority to accept or modify the terms of any order or contract, or to accept returns or cancellations of orders, or in any other way to make any binding commitments for PRINCIPAL.

Thus, a commission agent is endowed with no power to bind the principal.

As in the case of a distributor appointment, normally the parties mutually agree upon the effective date of the agreement and its duration. The agreement can be terminated by reason of breach or insolvency on the part of the agent, or from any other cause set forth that would lead to the termination of a distributor agreement. Upon such termination, the agent is to return to the principal any unused promotional materials, or the principal shall be obliged to pay commissions with respect to sales orders placed by purchasers to customers through the agent prior to the effective date of termination that are accepted by the principal, and for which the principal is paid the full amount.

The general legal provisions of an agency appointment are generally parallel to those outlined above with respect to distributor appointments and would include a nonassignment provision, a waiver provision, a governing-law provision, an arbitration provision, and a provision stating that the written agreement constitutes the entire agreement between the parties and supersedes all prior agreement (written or oral) between the parties.

Checklists of clauses typically appearing in foreign distributor and agency appointments are set forth in Appendices A and B of this chapter.

APPENDIX A–CHECKLIST: MASTER FOREIGN DISTRIBUTOR APPOINTMENT

Article

Article	1	Definitions
Article	2	Distributor Grant ✓
Article	3	Distributor's Undertakings ✓
Article	4	Principal's Undertakings ✓
Article	5	Price and Payment
Article	6	Shipping–Title and Risk–Cancellation
Article	7	Warranty–No Consequential Damages–Indemnity ✓
Article	8	Term and Termination
Article	9	Assignment
Article	10	Waiver
Article	11	Entire Agreement
Article	12	Validity
Article	13	Notices
Article	14	U.S. Laws and Regulations -
Article	15	Governing Law ✓
Article	16	Arbitration
Schedule	I	Products
Schedule	II	Minimum Spare Parts Complements
Schedule	III	Minimum Purchase Quotas
Schedule	IV	Patents and Trademarks
Schedule	V	Discount on Price Lists

APPENDIX B–CHECKLIST: FOREIGN AGENCY APPOINTMENT

Article

Article	1	Appointment
Article	2	Territory
Article	3	Sales Territory
Article	4	Confidential Information
Article	5	Reports
Article	6	Visits to Agent Premises by Representatives of Principal
Article	7	Sales Literature

4

SPECIAL U.S. AND FOREIGN LEGAL ASPECTS OF SETTING UP NETWORK

FOREIGN DEALER LEGISLATION

A U.S. exporter appointing one or more foreign representatives should be aware that a great number of foreign countries have enacted special laws for the protection of agents and distributors. Thus, each foreign appointment should carefully be reviewed in the light of local law. The legal status of the appointee is particularly important in determining his rights on termination of the contract. In practice, this has probably been the most difficult aspect of distribution arrangements for an exporter (principal) accustomed to terminating a contract upon giving notice specified in the contract or, in the absence of such agreement, upon reasonable notice.

Distinctions between Distributor, Agent, and Dealer

For purposes of termination indemnification it is often crucial to determine whether the appointee is a "distributor" or an "agent." A distributor (i) buys and sells for its own account, making its profit on the markup; (ii) carries customers' credit and bears the economic risk of collections on all sales; (iii) usually warehouses and physically distributes the goods; (iv) frequently renders after-sale service; and (v) cannot legally bind the U.S. principal, since the distributor is merely a customer.

By way of contrast, a commission agent promotes an order from a foreign customer for acceptance by his principal, and upon collection of the purchase price the principal accrues a commission for the account of such commission agent. An agent (i) does not buy or sell for his own account; (ii) carries no customer's credit, since the sales are in the name of and for the account of the principal; (iii) does not warehouse or physically distribute the goods; and (iv) may contractually bind his principal, but only to a degree consistent with the expression of implied authority given him in the appointment. In most agency appointments the commission agent is vested with no authority to bind his principal in any way whatsoever.

The term "dealer" in many protective jurisdictions, in the legal sense, includes both a distributor or an agent, although in the business sense it usually connotes a distributor. In many Middle Eastern jurisdictions, the term "agent" is a legal term broadly connoting both commission agents and distributors.

As a generalization, a commission agent normally is entitled to a greater degree of protection than a distributor, the theory being that a distributor is an independent merchant with parity of bargaining power and capable of protecting his interests. A commission agent is likened more to an employee, as a selling instrument of his principal, and entitled to equitable remuneration upon termination.

Categories of Foreign Law

There are three general categories of foreign law encountered in dealing with the issue of dealer protection.

(i) *Common Law*: First, there is the traditional English or common law approach, under which parties to a contract may agree to any termination provisions which suit them. If a contract provides that it may be terminated on 30 days' notice on either side, that governs the matter. There are no paramount local laws or code provisions which would override the contract and give greater rights to the foreign appointee.

(ii) *Protective Law*: In a second and growing category of countries, laws have been enacted for the protection of commission agents or distributors, or both. Current major protection law jurisdictions include: Austria, Belgium, France, West Germany, Italy, Luxembourg, the Netherlands, Norway, Finland, Sweden, Switzerland, Jordan, Lebanon, Oman, Saudi Arabia, Brazil, Colombia, Ecuador, Puerto Rico, the Dominican Republic, Panama, Costa Rica, Guatemala, Honduras, El Salvador, and Nicaragua.

The form and scope of statutory protection vary widely from jurisdiction to jurisdiction, but the usual pattern is to give the appointee a right to indemnities or damages on the termination or nonrenewal of the relationship without "just cause." Some countries require formal registration of the appointment and regulate the timing and manner of the termination notice.

While local legislation can in some cases be avoided through careful contract drafting, there is a growing tendency to enact protective legislation of sweeping scope to make avoidance virtually impossible. Under most protective statutes, an appointee cannot waive his termination indemnities. A formal waiver or an indirect waiver through a choice of U.S. state governing law would not be enforceable, since those jurisdictions invariably regard local protection laws as an expression of strong public policy which may not be frustrated by private contract.

Remedies available to an "unjustly" terminated dealer vary greatly, and damages may be extremely high. Typically, the statutes provide that a wrongfully terminated dealer may recover damages based on seniority, local "good will" generated, profits, and on investments in facilities made in reasonable reliance upon a continuation of the relationship. Damages awarded frequently are in the order of the appointee's profits over the most recent three to five years. In a few protective jurisdictions (e.g., Costa Rica, Puerto Rico, Panama), the principal can be enjoined from contracting with a successor appointee pending settlement of the case. In these instances settlement is made on the basis of the current appointee's "nuisance value," namely his ability to close the market until the suit is settled.

(iii) *Labor Law*: In a third group of countries, particularly in Latin American jurisdictions, an *individual* dealer, when terminated, may have the right to claim indemnification under the labor laws of his jurisdiction. The terminated individual ordinarily would have to demonstrate the existence of an employer-employee relationship. Under current labor laws in effect in several Latin American jurisdictions, this could be quite difficult. The employer-employee relationship is generally defined in terms of the employer's right to control the activities of the employee, a right which a U.S. principal normally would not have with respect to any of its foreign appointees.

Even without a conventional employer-employee relationship, however, individuals acting as commercial representatives may be presumed to be employees under the labor laws of some jurisdictions. For example, under Article 285 of Mexico's Federal Labor Law, commercial agents, salesmen, company representatives, promotional agents, and similar agents are considered to be "employees" if their activity is of a permanent nature, unless they do not personally perform the work or intervene only in occasional transactions.

To illustrate the kinds of indemnities which may be owed under labor laws, a terminated commercial agent covered by Mexico's Federal Labor Law would, under Articles 50 and 289 of that law, be entitled to payment from its principal of (i) 20 times the average daily commission or profit made in the year preceding termination, for each year during which the relationship has been in existence; and (ii) an amount equal to three months' commissions or profits.

A U.S. principal normally can avoid potential liability under local labor laws by ensuring that it contracts with a business entity rather than with an individual in his personal capacity.[1]

Contractual Protective Measures

To avoid local labor laws a U.S. principal should endeavor to contract with an incorporated entity rather than an individual.

In some countries the U.S. principal might tailor the appointment largely to protect itself against local legislation. For example, German legislation protecting commission agents can be circumvented by specifying that the contract will be governed under the laws of a U.S. state. There is a sufficient nexus between the U.S. state (the source of the goods) and the contract for German courts to recognize such a governing law clause. Through such a clause the German agent would waive any rights he might have under German law.

In countries such as Belgium and Colombia, legislation protecting distributors does not apply if the principal permits a fixed-term contract to expire at the end of its term. Thus, a fixed-term contract should be entered into in these jurisdictions and renewed at the end of its term if the distributor is performing satisfactorily. More than two renewals, however, would be held, at least in Belgium, to convert such a fixed-term appointment into an indefinite-term contract within the scope of local protective legislation.

Since an appointee's damages are usually geared to his seniority it is advisable to make an initial trial appointment of short term, such as one year, thereby minimizing damages if the appointee's performance is unsatisfactory.

To avoid an inadvertent renewal through the principal's failure to give an appointee notice of nonrenewal,[2] the contract should provide for automatic expiration of the appointment at the end of the agreed term. The parties may always mutually agree to renew the contract before, or even after, its automatic expiration.

Since foreign protective legislation normally provides that no compensation will be due from the U.S. principal if it terminates or refuses to renew the agreement for justifiable reasons, each appointment should set forth in some detail all the obligations and undertakings of the local distributor or commission agent. More often than not the principal would wish to terminate an appointee primarily because of its poor performance. It is, therefore, advisable to set minimum annual sales quotas and service obligations in the agreement. If these sales quotas and obligations are commercially reasonable, failure to meet them arguably would provide the principal justifiable cause to terminate or not renew the contract.

To restrict an appointee's access to his local courts, the U.S. principal might stipulate U.S. law as governing and provide for compulsory arbitration of all contractual disputes under the rules of the International Chamber of Commerce (ICC), with arbitration to be conducted (in English) in the United States. Arbitration under the ICC rules is time consuming, expensive,[3] and would be particularly inconvenient for the foreign appointee. An appointee would be encouraged to settle in some countries where compulsory arbitration clauses are honored. Tribunals in some jurisdictions would not be preempted of jurisdiction by such a clause. Tribunals in the 57 countries[4] which are signatories to the 1958 New York Convention on the Recognition and Enforcement of Foreign Arbitral Awards, however, cannot accept jurisdiction if arbitration is mandated in the contract. In these countries, moreover, a U.S. award would be fully enforceable and, thus, more effective than a U.S. judgment.

Risk of an Unqualified Agent or Distributor in the Middle East

Aside from protective legislation, a major risk in the Middle East is the possible appointment of an unqualified agent or distributor. In most Middle Eastern countries, an agent or an appointee must be a local national or a legal entity wholly owned by local nationals and properly registered in the appropriate registrar as an agent. With respect to government contracts, some countries require that no agents or intermediaries be used; for example, in Iraq, Syria, and Algeria. Other countries, such as Kuwait, Abu Dhabi, and Saudi Arabia insist on the use of a local agent. When agents are permitted, they normally must be identified to the government agency and their commission disclosed by registering the contract, or by filing an affidavit or statement at the appropriate local registry.

Failure to abide by the above rules could result in a suspension of the principal's right to do business in that country. It is therefore essential that the principal verify the proposed Middle Eastern agent's or distributor's local credentials and carefully comply with all local registration and disclosure requirements.

APPOINTMENTS IN THE EUROPEAN COMMON MARKET

The Treaty of Rome establishing the European Economic Community (the "EEC")[5] prohibits, under Article 85(1), agreements or practices between two or more enterprises which restrict competition within the EEC and affect trade among the member states of the EEC. Distribution agreements containing any provisions which affect trade or restrict competition (such as grants of exclusivity, noncompetition clauses, and restrictions on territory) are, therefore, subject to and prohibited by the Treaty of Rome.

Under this regime the distinction between an agent and a "distributor" is a very important one. Article 86 applies to exclusive distributorships but not to agencies, since the relationship between principal and agent is not deemed "between enterprises" within the meaning of the article.

Article 85(3) of this treaty, however, permits the promulgation of exemptions from the application of Article 85(1), for agreements or practices which contribute to the production or distribution of goods or to the promotion of technical or economic progress. The EEC Commission has therefore promulgated regulations granting automatic "block" exemptions to both exclusive distribution agreements and exclusive purchasing agreements meeting certain criteria discussed below. The *de minimis* guidelines may be applied to take the agreement outside the scope of Article 85 if the relevant market share is small enough. These *de minimis* guidelines are outlined below.

De Minimis Guidelines

Many agreements will not be subject to the prohibitions of Article 85 under the *de minimis* guidelines. Under these guidelines agreements which have a negligible effect on competition due to the size of the parties and the market share of the contractual products will fall outside the scope of Article 85.[6] Agreements will be considered to have a negligible effect on competition if: (1) the products which are the subject of the agreement, and other products of the participating undertakings considered by consumers to be similar in character, price, or use, does not represent in a substantial part of the EEC more than 5 percent of the total market for such products; *and* (2) the aggregate annual sales of the parties (including both parent and subsidiary companies of the supplier and the distributor) do not exceed 50 million European units of account.

If both of these requirements are satisfied, under the *de minimis* guidelines, Article 85(1) should not apply, even if the exclusive distribution or purchasing agreement includes restrictions not permitted by Regulations 1983/83 and 1984/83. The *de minimis* guidelines, however, are predicated on a policy pronouncement of the EEC Commission which is not binding on the European Court of Justice.

Assuming the above *de minimis* guidelines cannot be met, the Treaty of Rome and the availability of exemption from its prohibition are of importance to U.S. exporters because the EEC Commission has clearly indicated that Article 85 will be applied to activities of foreign businesses that affect trade or commerce in the EEC. It is immaterial to the application of Article 85(1) that one of the parties is outside the EEC is the agreement produces sufficient effect within the EEC.

Distribution Agreements

The original exemption available to distribution agreements was EEC Commission Regulation 67/67.[7] Effective July 1, 1983, two regulations, Regulations 1983/83 (regarding exclusive distribution agreements) and 1984/83 (regarding exclusive purchasing agreements) replaced Regulation 67/67.[8] Although the new regulations are substantially similar to the old, there are several important provisions in the new regulations which are quite distinct, as described below.

Permissible Restrictions

The following restrictions may permissibly be included in exclusive distribution agreements under both Regulation 67/67 and the new Regulation 1983/83 without jeopardizing the availability of exemption from the application of Article 85(1).

1. *Noncompetition clauses.* The distributor may be prohibited from manufacturing or distributing products which compete with the contractual products during the term of the contract. Under Regulation 67/67, it was permissible for a noncompetition clause to extend for an additional year beyond the term of the contract. Noncompeti-

tion clauses have now, however, been restricted by Regulation 1983/83 to the term of the contract only.

2. *Export sales.* The distributor may be prohibited from soliciting customers for the contractual products outside its territory and from maintaining a branch or warehouse outside its territory. Note that it is not permissible, however, to prohibit the distributor from selling the contractual products to unsolicited customers outside its contractual territory within the EEC. Otherwise stated, the distributor must be permitted to make unsolicited export sales.

3. *Minimum purchases.* The distributor may be required to purchase a full line of the contractual products or to purchase minimum quantities of the contractual products.

4. *Trademarks.* The distributor may be required to sell the contractual products under trademarks or packed and presented as specified by the supplier.

5. *Promotion.* The distributor may be required, in order to promote sales, to advertise the contractual products; to maintain a sales network for the contractual products; to maintain a stock of contractual products; to employ staff having specialized or technical training for the contractual products.

New Restrictions Permissible

Regulation 1983/83 has also clarified the permissible nature of certain other restrictions by adding to the list of permissible restrictions the following:

1. *Exclusive Purchasing.* The exclusive distributor may be required to obtain the contractual goods for resale only from the other party (i.e., from the supplier as opposed to parallel distributors or other third parties).

2. *After-Sales Service.* The distributor may be required to provide customer (after-sales) service and guarantee or warranty service.

3. *Direct Sales.* The supplier may be prohibited from supplying the contractual goods to users in the contractual territory. In other words, "no direct sales" clauses are now clearly permitted, but this is the only clearly permissible restriction which may be placed on the supplying party in exclusive distribution agreements.

4. *Territory.* The distributor's territory may now be restricted to the entire EEC, instead of merely a part of or a member state within the EEC. (Formerly, the entire EEC was not a permissible exclusive territory for a distributor; this restriction was an effort to ensure some

availability to consumers of an alternate source for the contractual goods).

Prohibited Restrictions

Under Regulation 1983/83, the block exemption will not be available to exclusive distribution agreements which contain any restrictions that violate Article 85(1) and are not expressly permitted by Regulation 1983/83, such as:

1. *Reciprocal Agreements between Manufacturers.* Under Regulations 67/67, manufacturers of competing goods could not enter into reciprocal exclusive distribution agreements for those goods without losing block exemption protection. Under Regulation 1983/83, the definition of competing goods is expanded so that manufacturers may not now enter into reciprocal exclusive distribution agreements regarding identical goods or any other goods which are considered by users as equivalent in view of their characteristics, price, and intended use. The definition of a manufacturer of competing goods has also been expanded to include parties with controlled or controlling affiliates that manufacture competing products. Moreover, Regulation 1983/83 does not offer block exemption protection to reciprocal distribution agreements between parties manufacturing competing goods if the distribution is *nonexclusive* as to one party, unless the total annual sales of at least one party to the agreement (including sales of controlled or controlling affiliates) are less than 100 million European units of account.[9]

2. *Restraints on Intrabrand Competition.* Under both Regulations 67/67 and 1983/83, the block exemption is not available if the parties take measures to restrict the availability of the contractual goods to either dealers or consumers. Such restrictions may be found either in the text of the agreement or the manner of implementation of the agreement. The regulations note as a specific instance of such a restraint the use of industrial property rights to prevent sales in the contractual territory. Under Regulation 67/67 the exclusion applied only if both parties to the agreement took measures in this regard. Regulation 1983/83 prohibits any such action by either of the parties. Also, Regulation 1983/83 prohibits such measures even if taken with regard to sales from sources outside the EEC if no alternative sources of supply are available within the EEC.

Restrictions Newly Prohibited under Regulation 1983/83

Regulation 1983/83 has introduced a new exclusion, under which the block exemption will not be available if, notwithstanding the provisions contained in the text of the agreement, consumers of the contractual goods can, as a practical matter, obtain the contractual goods only from the exclusive distributor and have no alternative source of supply outside the contractual territory. This would be the case where, for example, the supplier is enforcing a policy of absolute territorialism; that is, the supplier places an export prohibition on all of the distributors in its distribution network. In such a case, a distribution agreement would not benefit from the exemption, even though on the face of the agreement there may be nothing indicating the unavailability to users of alternate sources of supply. This new exclusion, which appears to be somewhat duplicative of the restriction discussed immediately above, was placed in Regulation 1983/83 to counterbalance the effect of the new permission which allows distributors to have the entire EEC as their territory.

Withdrawal of Exemption

It should be noted that the EEC Commission reserves the right, under both old Regulation 67/67 and new Regulation 1983/83, to withdraw the availability of the block exemption when, notwithstanding the fact that the text of agreement contains no impermissible restrictions, (i) there is no "effective competition" in the goods in the contractual territory, (ii) other suppliers have difficulty effecting distribution within the contractual territory, or (iii) the exclusive distributor sells the contractual goods at excessively high prices or refuses to supply categories of purchasers who cannot obtain the goods elsewhere or applies price discrimination to such purchasers.

Exclusive Purchasing Agreements

Formerly, both exclusive distribution and exclusive purchasing agreements were covered by the same EEC regulation (Regulation 67/67). Effective July 1, 1983, however, exclusive purchasing agreements are the subject of a separate regulation, Regulation 1984/83.

The EEC Commission considers an exclusive purchasing agreement to be one under which a distributor undertakes to purchase certain goods for resale only from a given supplier, without obtaining from the supplier a grant of exclusivity with regard to a specific territory in return. Thus, if a distributor is to be an *exclusive* distributor, the availability of a block exemption (and the permissibility of an exclusive purchasing requirement) is governed by Regulation 1983/83. If the distributor is to be *nonexclusive*, and yet the goods are to be purchased only from the supplier, Regulation 1984/83 governs. If the distributor is to be nonexclusive and there are to be no restrictions imposed on supplier or the distributor, there would arguably be no restrictions which need to be exempted from the application of Article 85(1) of the Treaty of Rome, and thus neither Regulation 1983/83 nor 1984/83 would apply.

Regulation 1984/83 exempts from the application of Article 85(1) agreements between two (but not more than two) parties whereby one party (the nonexclusive distributor or "purchaser") agrees to purchase certain goods for resale only from the other party (the "supplier") or from one of the supplier's affiliates or distributors. Additionally, the agreements subject to Regulation 1984/83 are distribution agreements under which purchases are made for resale. Regulation 1984/83 does not apply to "requirements contracts," i.e., exclusive purchasing for end-use. Regulation 1984/83 also contains specific provisions regarding beer supply and service station contracts, but since these provisions are not of general applicability they will not be discussed here.

Territory

Since by definition the purchaser is not exclusive, it will not have an exclusive territory. Regulation 1984/83 therefore speaks in terms of the "principal sales area" given to the purchaser.

Permissible Restrictions

The following restrictions may permissibly be included in exclusive purchasing agreements without jeopardizing the availability of the block exemption under Regulation 1984/83:

1. *Exclusive Purchasing.* The purchaser may be required to purchase the contractual goods for resale only from the supplier or from one of the supplier's affiliates or distributors.

2. *Minimum Purchases.* The purchaser may be required to purchase minimum quantities of goods, which are subject to the exclusive purchasing obligations, as well as to purchase a full line of the products.

3. *Trademark.* The purchaser may be required to sell the contractual products under trademarks or packed and presented as specified by the supplier.

4. *Sales Promotion.* The purchaser may be required, in order to promote sales, to advertise the contractual products; to maintain a sales network for the contractual products; to provide customer (after-sale) and guarantee service; and to employ staff having specialized or technical training for the contractual products.

5. *Supplier's Direct Sales.* The supplier may be prohibited from directly selling the contractual goods in the purchaser's "principal sales area" and at the purchaser's level of distribution. For example, if the purchaser sells to retailers, the supplier could not be prohibited from making direct sales to end-users.

Prohibited Restrictions

A block exemption under Regulation 1984/83 will not be available to exclusive purchasing agreements which contain any restrictions that violate Article 85(1) and are not expressly permitted by Regulation 1984/83 such as:

1. *Export Sales.* In contrast to Regulations 67/67 and 1983/83, the purchaser in an exclusive purchasing agreement may not be prohibited from soliciting or effecting export sales or from establishing a distribution network throughout the EEC, even if the purchaser has been given a "principal sales area" in which to operate.

2. *Reciprocal Agreements between Manufacturers.* A provision similar to that described above for Regulation 1983/83 is included in 1984/83, thus making the block exemption unavailable to exclusive purchasing agreements between manufacturers.

3. *Products.* The exemption is not available to exclusive purchasing agreements which cover more than one type of good, unless the goods are connected by their nature or commercial usage.

4. *Duration.* In contrast to exclusive distribution agreements, an exclusive purchasing agreement will not be eligible for the block exemption if it has a fixed term of longer than five years. While the subject of renewals is not explicitly covered by Regulation 1984/83, renewals for fixed periods only, rather than for an indefinite term, are much more likely to fall within the scope of the exemption.

Withdrawal of Exemption

The EEC Commission has reserved the right to withdraw the availability of the block exemption with regard to any exclusive purchasing agreement when, notwithstanding the fact that the text of the agreement contains no impermissible restrictions, (i) there is no "effective competition" in the goods in the contractual territory, (ii) other suppliers have difficulty effecting distribution within the contractual territory, (iii) the supplier refuses to supply categories of resellers who cannot obtain the contractual goods elsewhere, or applies differing sales terms to them without objective justification, or (iv) the supplier applies less favorable terms to its exclusive purchaser customers than to its other customers at the same level of distribution.

Effective Date and Transition Period

Although Regulations 1983/83 and 1984/83 were "effective" on July 1, 1983, Regulation 67/67 will continue to apply to both exclusive distribution and exclusive purchasing contracts until December 31, 1986 if the agreements are in force on July 1, 1983. Thus, the parties to agreements in force by December 31, 1983 have until December 31, 1986 to modify agreements which conform to Regulation 67/67 but which do not conform to the new regulations. Agreements which entered into force after January 1, 1984 must comply with the new regulations.

U.S. FOREIGN CORRUPT PRACTICES ACT

A U.S. exporter must takes steps to assure that at all times it is in compliance with Section 30A of the Securities Exchange Act of 1934, as amended by the Foreign Corrupt Practices Act of 1977 (the "Act"). This discussion does not deal with the books and records and internal controls provisions of the Act, but clearly these provisions, which now comprise Section 13(b)(2) of the Securities Exchange Act, must be considered with the corrupt payment proscriptions of the Act (discussed below) in devising an effective compliance program.

Illegal Foreign Payments

By way of general background, the Act imposes civil and criminal liability[10] on corporations and their officers, directors, employees, shareholders, and agents for (i) their corrupt use of interstate facilities or the mails to further a wrongful intent to induce a foreign official to misuse his official position or to use his influence with a foreign government, (ii) by paying or offering, promising, or authorizing payments of money or other things of value to such an official, in order (iii) to assist in obtaining or retaining business for the corporation or directing business to others. The Act also covers similar payments to foreign political parties or party officials and candidates for foreign office.

This is a slightly different, but no less direct, proscription of the corrupt payment section of the Act. This section prohibits the corrupt use of commerce or the mails by the same persons to further a payment or offer, promise or authorization of a payment to *anyone*,[11] when the person knows *or has reason to know* that all, or part of the payment, directly or indirectly, will be offered, given, or promised to a foreign official, political party, party official, or candidate for foreign office for the same proscribed purposes. It is in the context of this prohibition under the Act that an exporter's concern with commission or other payments to foreign agents and distributors arises.

Reason to Know

The facts and circumstances discussed below bear on the "reason to know" standard. These circumstances have been identified by the Securities and Exchange Commission in its report to the Proxmire Committee[12] as ones which may suggest that improper or illegal payments are or will be made. It is obviously advisable that a U.S. corporation which sells overseas through independent foreign businessmen be sensitive to such circumstances, so when one or more of them is present, the corporation will take steps to prevent any payment or other illegal activity from occurring.

"Reason to know" in the criminal context probably means, at least, that a company, through its officers, was conscious of, but disregarded, circumstances indicative of bribery by a third person. Such circumstances, in which a company fails to take appropriately diligent procedures to determine that a payment will not be made or to prevent such a payment, may well result in liability. Moreover, although it may be possible for senior management of U.S. companies and the companies themselves to avoid criminal liability under the payment provisions of the Act by demonstrating that, notwithstanding some procedures designed to avoid or at least to detect such circumstances, they in fact had no knowledge of facts suggesting a bribe by a foreign sales agent, they may still be unable to avoid civil liability under the Act. The Securities and Exchange Commission takes the position that a demonstration of simple negligence is sufficient under the Act to obtain injunctive relief. In addition, depending upon the nature and extent of the company's internal procedures, there may also be found a violation of the internal controls requirement of the Act.

The circumstances which may raise an inference of illegal bribes by foreign sales representatives, agents, or distributors (or other third persons) and which may constitute "reason to know" of such bribes by U.S. companies are discussed below.

Reputation of the Country Involved

Some countries, such as Nigeria and Indonesia, have a known reputation for corruption and bribery. A U.S. principal, thus, automatically should be "on guard" and should adopt appropriately diligent procedures with respect to payments to local agents in these jurisdictions.

Reputation of Agent

If the agent under consideration for appointment has a known record of prior misconduct, appropriate diligent procedures should be adopted to reasonably assure the U.S. principal that misconduct in the context of the current appointment would be highly unlikely.

Agent's Refusal to Provide Representations

A refusal to provide contractual representations concerning payments to government officials normally would constitute cause for not appointing or for terminating a foreign agent; but in many countries, including all countries in the Middle East, an agency appointment is registered with the Ministry of Commerce and Industry and made a matter of public record. An agent in these countries will often express concern that a public contractual covenant concerning bribery is a reflection upon his integrity. In this instance a contemporaneous written side commitment from the agent, executed in conjunction with the agency appointment, would be appropriate.

Relationship to Government Officials

If the representative or any of its principals, employees, or consultants is an official of a government of any jurisdiction in the representative's territory (or any governmental subdivision, agency, instrument, corporation, or other government-related entity) or a party official or candidate, or is related, by blood or marriage, to such person, an inference could be made that such persons may have a direct or indirect interest in payments made to the representative in connection with sales to the government. Such facts, therefore, require further investigation so that a U.S. company can be assured that either such relationship is benign, in that it is not likely to be a factor in government procurement, or the government or party official or candidate is not in fact sharing, directly or indirectly, in any commission or fee to be paid by the company to the representative.

Under the Act it is at least arguable that payments may be made to government officials who act on behalf of a foreign company's sales representatives in connection with sales to units of government with which such official is unconnected. Nevertheless, U.S. companies obviously must be made aware of all the facts before they can be in a position to assess whether, in any given circumstances, a government official's relationship with their sales representative is, in fact, one which does not suggest that payments will be made to obtain government business.[13]

Size of Commission Payments

If a sales representative's commission rate is or is proposed to be in excess of the "going rate" in the country in question or will result in payments of substantial absolute amounts in light of the services to be rendered by the representative, this may suggest that the representative may intend to pass on a portion of the commission to the customers. In the case of government sales, such circumstances may, therefore, constitute "reason to know" that an illegal payment to obtain government business is intended. (In the case of private sales, the same circumstances could suggest that the representative is engaging in commercial bribery. Although foreign commercial bribery is not proscribed by the Act, in addition to a company's need to consider its disclosure under U.S. securities laws, it is clearly the position of the Federal Trade Commission that foreign commercial bribery may constitute a violation of Section 5 of the Federal Trade Commission Act.)

Companies should be alert to any local practice under which "going" commission rates are determined to some degree by the size of the underlying sale. For example, although it may be confirmed that 5 percent is the "going" rate, further inquiry may show that this rate is reduced as the size of any given underlying sale increases. Also, any variation between the kind and quantity of services typically furnished by local representatives of foreign companies selling products or equipment similar to one company's and those proposed to be furnished to that company by its representative should be reflected in the rate of commission to which that company's representative is entitled.

The place and manner of payment of commissions may also be relevant to the question of whether a sales representative is passing a portion of the payment on to a government or political official. Companies should therefore be alert to requests for payment to third parties or to bank accounts identified by number only or in countries that have no apparent connection with the underlying transaction.

Nature of Services

If in fact the nature of the services which a company expects a foreign sales representative to furnish is substantially different from that typically expected of sales representatives or agents, a full explanation should be provided to members of senior management so that a judgment can be made as to whether the circumstances constitute reason to know the representative may intend to make proscribed payments. This is particularly important if a sales agent's function is merely "to introduce" a company or its local sales representative or dealer to potential customers.

In many jurisdictions, "intermediation" or "finders" services fees are legally permissible. Nevertheless, particularly in the context of large government projects, which often are the subject of broad international tender, the employment of intermediaries and the payment of substantial fees to them raise a sufficiently serious question under the Act that closer examination of such relationships should be required at the outset.

Assuming that a company is satisfied that such an intermediary can be appointed in a particular circumstance, it is essential that the related contract clearly and accurately describe the mediation services which such a company expects the intermediary to provide, and that it contain stringent negative covenants as to the intermediary's activities. Nothing may appear as damaging in retrospect (however proper the services actually rendered are) as a contract providing for a "laundry list" of services to be provided by an agent, but which the agent in fact does not perform or indeed is incapable of performing.

Over-Invoicing

Any suggestion by a representative that a company submit for payment invoices in amounts greater than the true price of the equipment sold, the difference to be rebated elsewhere, suggests that the representative (if acting as a distributor) or the end-customer may be evading local tax or exchange control laws. In addition, over-invoicing can suggest that a bribe or other corrupt payment has been or will be made in that it often is accompanied by uncertainty as to the actual recipients of the rebate. Moreover, quite apart from the proscriptions of the Act, the Justice Department has taken the position that in certain circumstances over-invoicing may constitute a violation of U.S. mail or wire fraud statutes.

In light of the risks involved, a company should always employ reasonable care in connection with entering into new relationships with overseas agents and distributors. Appropriately diligent investigation procedures should be developed and observed to confirm the good reputation and integrity of all agents and distributors, particularly those which are likely to bring material business to the company. The appropriate degree of thoroughness of such investigations may vary depending on the surrounding circumstances. Furthermore, the company's employees should understand that any unusual or suspicious aspects of the manner in which a foreign representative conducts or proposes to conduct his business should be promptly reported to the company's counsel for evaluation.

NOTES

1. On rare occasions, however, labor law indemnities could be payable by the principal even if the appointee is a business entity. For example, under Article 15 of the Mexican Federal Labor Law, if a legal entity performs services *exclusively or principally* for another, and does not have sufficient resources to satisfy its labor law obligations to its employees, the beneficiary enterprise, i.e., the U.S. principal, would be jointly and severally liable for labor obligations owed to the employees of the appointee.

2. In many agreements, for example, the contract is automatically renewed unless the principal gives notice of nonrenewal 90-180 days prior to expiration. Failure to give notice would renew the contract and increase damages payable to an unsatisfactory appointee.

3. Arbitrators' fees and administrative costs, payable in advance by the parties could be $15,000-$30,000, depending upon the complexity of the case and the amount in issue.

4. Countries included are all major European trading partners of the United States; Chile, Colombia, Ecuador, and Mexico in Latin America; Egypt, Israel, Jordan, Kuwait, Syria, and Tunisia in the Middle East; and Indonesia, Japan, Korea, the Philippines, Sir Lanka, and Thailand in the Far East.

5. The ten members of the EEC are Belgium, Luxembourg, the Netherlands, France, West Germany, Italy, Ireland, the United Kingdom, Denmark, and Greece. Portugal and Spain are currently seeking admission.

6. *Off. J. Comm. Eur.* (No. L 63) (1970), amended December 9, 1977.

7. *Off. J. Comm. Eur.* (No. 57) 849 (1969), amended by *Off. J. Comm. Eur.* (No. L 276) (1972).

8. *Off. J. Comm. Eur.* (No. L 173) (1983).

9. One E.C.U. is currently equal to approximately one U.S. dollar.

10. Penalties include fines of up to $1 million for a business entity and up to five-year felony jail terms and/or $10,000 fines for individuals.

11. The Act has been construed to cover distributors as well as agents. Distributors are deemed to receive a profit-making opportunity (dealer markup), all or part of which may be passed on to a foreign government official.

12. Report of the Securities and Exchange Commission on Questionable and Illegal Corporate Payment and Practices to Senate Banking, Housing, and Urban Affairs Committee, May 12, 1976.

13. In the context of their disclosure obligations under U.S. law, companies, of course, need also be concerned about the legality of any relationship between a government official and a sales representative or agent under local law.

5

SPECIAL U.S. LEGAL
ASPECTS OF EXPORTING

U.S. EXPORT CONTROLS

The centerpiece of the U.S. program of export control is the Export Administration Act,[1] most recently amended and reenacted in 1979, and the Export Administration Regulations[2] issued thereunder.[3] The Export Administration Act authorizes the president to impose controls on U.S. exports in order: (a) to restrict the export of goods and technology which would make a significant contribution to the military potential of any other country or combination of countries which would prove detrimental to the national security of the United States;[4] (b) to restrict the export of goods and technology where necessary to further significantly the foreign policy of the United States or to fulfill its declared international obligations;[5] and (c) to restrict the export of goods where necessary to protect the domestic economy from the excessive drain of scarce materials and to reduce the serious inflationary impact of foreign demand.[6]

Export Licensing Procedures

The means by which these export controls are implemented is a licensing procedure, administered by the Office of Export Administration of the Department of Commerce.[7] All exports of commodities and technical data from the United States to any destination other than Canada require an export license from the Department of Commerce. Those commodities which are not deemed to have strategic applications or to be in short supply, and which are not subject to foreign policy controls, may be exported under *general licenses*.[8] General licenses, of which the most important for commodity exports is the general license G-DEST, are established by specific provisions of the Export Administration Regulations. As a result, there is no need for an exporter to make a formal application to the Office of Export Administration for a license for each specific export transaction involving commodities which are subject to general license requirements. Instead, the fact that the commodities are exported under authority of a general license is noted on the documentation (the Shipper's Export Declaration) for the export transaction.

In contrast, a validated, or specific transaction, license is required (i) for the export to some or all foreign destinations of strategic commodities and unpublished technical data relating to certain of those commodities; (ii) for the export to all destinations of commodities deemed to be in short supply; and (iii) for the export of commodities and technical data which are subject to foreign policy export controls to the countries that are the targets of those controls.[9] The validated licensing procedure permits the Department of Commerce Office of Export Administration to review proposed exports of controlled or restricted commodities and technical data on a case-by-case basis, in order to ensure that each such proposed export (i) will not make a significant contribution to the military potential of another country to the detriment of U.S. national security; and (ii) is consistent with U.S. foreign policy objectives.[10]

The determination of whether a validated license is required for the export of specific commodities to a specific destination is made by reference to the Commodity Control List, which is published as Supplement No. 1 to § 399.1 of the Export Administration Regulations.[11] The Commodity Control List classifies all commodities that require a validated license for export to some or all destinations into one of the following categories: (i) metal-working machinery; (ii) chemical and petroleum equipment; (iii) electrical and power-generating equipment; (iv) general industrial equipment; (v) transportation equipment; (vi) electronics and precision instruments; (vii) metals, minerals, and their manufacturers; (viii) chemicals, metalloids, petroleum products, and related materials; (ix) rubber and rubber products; and (x) miscellaneous. The nations of the world are classified into various country groups, which are set forth in Table 5.1. With respect to each controlled commodity, the Commodity Control List indicates the country group or groups for which a validated export license is required. Thus, for example, integrated circuits and other micropro-

Table 5.1

Country Group	Countries	Comments
Canada	Canada	Almost all goods and technical data, except goods and technical data relating to nuclear weaponry, are exportable without an export license
Country Group T	Western Hemisphere (except Cuba)	Validated license required for export of some goods and technical data subject to national security controls and for export of crime control and detection equipment
Country Group V	Western Europe, Middle East, Africa, non-Communist Asia, China (after November 23, 1983)	Special antiterrorism controls on exports to Syria and South Yemen; special human rights controls on exports to South Africa and Namibia; special controls on exports to Afghanistan to prevent diversion to USSR; validated license required for export of crime control and detection equipment to all destinations except NATO, Japan, Australia, New Zealand
Country Group P	People's Republic of China (prior to November 23, 1983)	
Country Group Q	Romania	
Country Group W	Poland, Hungary	
Country Group Y	Soviet Union, East Germany, Czechoslovakia, Mongolia, Bulgaria, Albania	Between 1/4/82 and 11/13/82, restrictions on exports to USSR: prohibition on export of oil and gas exploration, drilling, transmission, and refining equipment; validated licenses for exports to U.S.S.R. denied

61

Table 5.1 (continued)

Country Group	Countries	Comments
Country Group S	Libya	As of 3/12/82 validated license required for export of all commodities and technical data, except food and medical supplies, to Libya. License applications for export of high-tech and oil field equipment and technical data will be denied
Country Group Z	North Korea, Cuba, Vietnam, Cambodia	Almost absolute embargo on export of U.S. goods and technical data to these destinations

cessor semiconductors are classified as Item 1564 on the Commodity Control List, which indicates that a validated license is required for the export of such commodities to all destinations (i.e., to all country groups), except Canada. Similarly, electronic computers and related components and peripherals, which are classified as Item 1565 on the Commodity Control List, require a validated license for export to all destinations, except Canada.

In recognition of the problems and delays that may arise as the result of the requirements of an individual validated license for each shipment of commodities that are subject to export controls, the Export Administration Regulations establish special commodity licensing procedures, the most important of which are (i) project licenses and (ii) distribution licenses, where 25 or more individual validated licenses would otherwise be required.[12] The project licensing procedure permits an exporter to export specified goods and/or technical data for a period of one year (subject to renewal for up to two years) for specified activities, such as the construction or expansion of a major facility or supplying maintenance, repair, and operating materials to an existing facility abroad.[13] The distribution license permits an exporter to make repeated shipments of restricted goods over a period of one year (also subject to renewal for up to two years) to approved foreign consignees under an international marketing program.[14] In order to be approved by the Office of Export Administration for purposes of a distribution license, the exporter's consignees must be (i) branches, subsidiaries, or affiliates of the exporter; (ii) foreign distributors with whom the exporter has written agreements which assure compliance with the Export Administration Regulations and which specify the countries in which the goods are to be sold; or (iii) end-users purchasing the goods in question for their own use or use in the manufacture of other goods.[15] Distribution licenses will be issued only for exports to consignees in the Western Hemisphere (except Cuba), Western Europe, the Middle East, non-Communist Asia (including Australia and New Zealand), and Africa.[16]

During the past two years, export control enforcement authorities in the Department of Commerce, the Department of Defense, and the Customs Service have expressed their concern that the distribution license special licensing procedure does not provide for sufficient controls against diversion or re-export of U.S. commodities to restricted destinations (e.g., Eastern Europe and the Soviet Union). As a result, on January 19, 1984, the Office of Export Administration issued proposed regulations which, if ultimately adopted as final regulations, would substantially restrict the availability and use of distribution licenses.[17] Under the proposed regulations, distribution licenses would be available only for U.S. exporters that can demonstrate that they obtained at least 50 individual validated licenses during the preceding year, and the class of consignees eligible for exports under a distribution license would be limited to those foreign firms with which the U.S. exporter/licensee has been doing business for a period of at least one year prior to the date of application for the distribution license. The proposed regulations would also impose significant administrative burdens on foreign distributors that receive U.S. goods under a distribution license. On sales of controlled commodities outside its country of residence, a foreign distributor under a distribution license would be required to obtain certifications from its customers against unauthorized re-export or diversion. Moreover, each foreign distributor would be required to provide the U.S. Office of Export Administration with a list of its anticipated customers for controlled U.S. commodities on a quarterly basis. Finally, the proposed regulations would add a number of commodities to the list of goods that may not be exported under a distribution license.

The proposed regulations have evoked a storm of protest among firms that export controlled commodities under distribution licenses. At this point, the Office of Export Administration is reviewing the proposed regulations in light of the substantial volume of negative comments. It should be anticipated that new, somewhat more restrictive regulations governing the distribution licenses will be issued by the Office of Export Administration, but at this point it is impossible to predict the final form of such regulations.

Technical Data Export Controls

The controls embodied in the Export Administration Regulations apply not only to exports of commodities, but also to exports of technical data. For purposes of these export controls, technical data include:[18]

> Information of any kind that can be used, or adapted for use in the design, production, manufacture, utilization or reconstruction of articles or materials. The data may take a tangible form, such as a model, prototype, blueprint, or an operating manual; or they may take an intangible form such as technical service.

It should be specifically noted that unbundled computer software is deemed to be technical data for purposes of export control.

As indicated above, all exports of U.S. technical data must be effected under either a general license or a validated license. It should be emphasized that the concept of an "export" of technical data is considerably broader than simply the shipment of documents embodying technical data to foreign destinations. Export of technical data is deemed to have occurred when such information is made available to nonresident foreign nationals by oral communications within the United States or by visual inspection of facilities and equipment in the United States. Thus, a validated license may be required in order for a U.S. engineer to present a paper, discussing restricted technology, at a seminar at which nonresidents will be in attendance. Similarly a validated license may be required to permit nonresident foreign nationals to tour a U.S. manufacturing facility in which restricted manufacturing processes are used. The concept of an "export" of U.S. technical data also includes the application abroad of technical information and experience learned in the United States. Thus, a validated technical data export license may be required in order to dispatch a U.S. engineer or technician abroad to assist a foreign customer.[19]

The relevant section of the Export Administration Regulations, § 379, provides for two types of general technical data export licenses, GTDA and GTDR, and identifies the technical data for which validated licenses are required for export to some or all destinations. The general license GTDA permits the export *to all destinations*, without specific authorization from the Office of Export Administration, of technical data that are freely available to the public in libraries, etc., or that can be obtained at nominal cost.[20] Most other technical data that are not in the public domain, including proprietary information about manufacturing and industrial processes, may be exported to *noncommunist* destinations under a general license GTDR, subject, in some cases, to the requirement that the foreign consignee provide written assurance that neither the data, nor the *direct foreign-produced product* thereof, will be re-exported to a communist country without specific authorization from the Office of Export Administration.[21] In this context, it should be noted that on June 6, 1983 the Office of Export Administration issued amendments to the Export Administration Regulations, which confirm that written assurance against unauthorized re-export is required for the export of *all computer software* under general license GTDR.[22] It should be emphasized that the general license GTDR is the most important license for technical data exports to noncommunist destinations, and is available for all such exports, except the fairly narrow categories of technical data specified in § § 379.4(c) and (d) of the regulations, for which validated licenses are required.[23]

In contrast, the general license GTDR is generally not available for technical data exports to communist countries.[24] Under § 379.4(b) of the regulations, technical data may be exported to a communist country under a general license GTDR *only* if the data:[25]

(i) are exported in conjunction with, and are directly related to, commodities which have been licensed for export to the particular communist destination;

(ii) are exported within one year of the date of export of the commodities to which they relate;

(iii) are of a type customarily delivered in conjunction with the commodities in question;

(iv) are necessary to the assembly, installation, maintenance, repair, or operation of the commodities; and

(v) are not related to production, manufacture, or construction of the commodities.

Apart from transactions which satisfy all of the foregoing conditions, a validated license is required for essentially all technical data exports (except technical data in the public domain) to any communist country. Thus, a U.S. computer manufacturer may be able to export object-coded software to a communist country consignee under a general license GTDR, in conjunction with the export of a computer to that consignee for which a validated license has been obtained.[26] By contrast, a validated license must be obtained for the export of "unbundled" software (whether source coded or object coded) to a communist country consignee.

The Office of Export Administration is currently reviewing and revising the provisions of the Export Administration Regulations (§ 379) governing technical data exports. No proposed revised technical data regulations have, as yet, been issued, but there is some reason to believe that revised technical data controls, when issued, will introduce new restrictions on technical data exports, particularly technical data utilized in the manufacture of semiconductor devices.

Authorization Requirements for the Re-export of U.S. Commodities and Technical Data

A principal source of controversy regarding the export controls embodied in the Export Administration Regulations is their broad extraterritorial scope. Thus, authorization of the Office of Export Administration is required not only for direct exports of commodities or technical data from the United States, but also for the *re-export* from one foreign destination to another of U.S. origin commodities or technical data, *and* for the export from one foreign destination to another of the direct foreign-produced product of U.S. technical data.[27] Indeed, the 1982 prohibitions on the sale of oil and gas equipment and technical data to the Soviet Union extended not only to the export and re-export of U.S. commodities and technical data and to the direct foreign-produced product of U.S. technical data, but also to transactions by foreign affiliates of U.S. corporations, even if the commodities or technical data were entirely of foreign origin.[28]

Although Office of Export Administration re-export authorization is required for transfers of U.S. commodities or technical data from one foreign destination to another, in most cases specific approval for proposed re-export transactions is not required. Sections 374.2 and 379.8(b) identify a series of circumstances in which authorization to re-export commodities or technical data exists by mandate of the regulations (analogous to a general license for direct exports). In effect, specific re-export authorization is required only for those transfers of U.S. commodities or technical data (or direct products of such technical data) for which a validated license would be required if the goods or technical data were exported directly from the United States to the prospective consignee.[29]

Licensing Policy

The validated licensing procedure is the means by which the Office of Export Administration can review, on a transaction by transaction basis, proposed exports of restricted commodities and technical data. Whether a proposed export will in fact be authorized depends on the Office of Export Administration's current export policy with respect to the commodities or technical data in question and the proposed destination. Thus, for example, for proposed exports of most restricted commodities and technical data to destinations in Western Europe, Latin America, Africa, and non-Communist Asia, it is the general policy of the Office of Export Administration to *grant* validated licenses, unless there is reason to believe that the commodities or technical data will be diverted from the end-use or destination stated in the validated license application.[30] In effect, subject to appropriate safeguards against diversion or re-export to a communist country, or (with respect to limited categories of goods and technical data) to a noncommunist country which is subject to foreign policy export controls, it is generally possible to obtain authorization to export almost all commodities and technical data to Western industrial and commercial countries.

There is considerably greater likelihood that applications for validated licenses to export controlled commodities to restricted destinations, such as the Soviet Union or the communist countries of Eastern Europe, will be denied.[31] The regulations indicate that applications for validated licenses to export controlled commodities to the Soviet Union or Eastern Europe will be granted where the Office of Export Administration, in conjunction with the Department of Defense, determines that the commodities or technical data proposed for export will not make a significant contribution to the military potential of the country of destination, in a manner that would prove detrimental to U.S. national security.[32] Thus, many high-tech commodities that are exportable to Western destinations (albeit under a validated license) are not exportable to the Soviet Union or Eastern Europe.

Export licensing policy with respect to the People's Republic of China stands in marked contrast to the licensing policy with respect to the Soviet Union and Eastern Europe. In recent years, U.S. export policy with respect to China has become increasingly liberal.[33] Most recently, on November 23, 1983, the Office of Export Administration issued amendments to the regulations by which China was reclassified from Country Group P to Country Group V for export control purposes.[34] Thus, for proposed exports to China of most controlled commodities, the review of license applications will be based on the risk of diversion to unauthorized uses or potentially hostile destinations (e.g., North Korea), rather than the possible contribution to Chinese military potential. In that sense, the export control policy with respect to China is more closely akin to the policy for Western Europe, Africa, the Middle East, and non-Communist Asia than it is to the export control policy for other communist countries. It should be emphasized, however, that there remain a number of important distinctions between export licensing requirements for China and export licensing requirements for noncommunist countries. For example, distribution licenses are not available for the export of controlled commodities to China. Similarly, a validated license will continue to be required for the export of proprietary technical data to China, whereas most technical data can be exported to other Country Group V destinations under general license GTDR.

COCOM Approval

The United States participates in a program of multinational export control, along with Belgium, Canada, Denmark, France, West Germany, Greece, Italy, Japan, Luxembourg, the Netherlands, Norway, Portugal, Turkey, and the United Kingdom.[35] This system of multinational controls is administered by an informal Coordinating Committee (COCOM), which reviews proposed exports of multilaterally controlled commodities (commodities identified by the code letter "A" on the Commodity Control List) to consignees in Eastern Europe, the Soviet Union, and the People's Republic of China. Thus, even after the United States government has tentatively approved a proposed export of an "A" item to one of the foregoing destinations, the proposed export transaction must be reviewed and approved by COCOM before the Office of Export Administration will issue a validated license, authorizing shipment of the goods in question.[36]

Foreign Policy Export Controls

The most controversial aspect of U.S. export controls are those restrictions that have been imposed to achieve foreign policy objectives. The fundamental concept underlying foreign policy controls on U.S. exports is to exert pressure on a foreign nation to abandon policies or activities which are deemed to be contrary to the foreign policy interests and objectives of the United States by denying that nation access to certain U.S. goods and technical data. Since restriction of U.S. exports also implies a loss to the U.S. economy of the benefits of exporting, such foreign policy export controls are not without substantial costs.[37] Moreover, extraterritorial foreign policy export controls may strain otherwise friendly relations between the United States and its principal allies and trading partners. In recognition of these facts, in reenacting the Export Administration Act in 1979, Congress directed that export controls for foreign policy purposes be reviewed annually and be extended or modified and new controls be imposed *only* after full consideration of the following factors:[38]

(1) the probability that such controls will achieve the intended foreign policy purpose, in light of other factors, including *the availability from other countries of the goods or technology* proposed for such controls;

(2) the compatibility of the proposed controls with the foreign policy objectives of the United States, including the effort to counter

international terrorism, and with overall United States policy toward the country which is the proposed target of the controls;

(3) *the reaction of other countries* to the imposition or expansion of such export controls by the United States;

(4) the *likely effects* of the proposed controls *on the export performance of the United States*, on the competitive position of the United States in the international economy, on the international reputation of the United States as a supplier of goods and technology, and on individual U.S. companies and their employees and communities, including the effects of the controls on existing contracts;

(5) the *ability of the United States to enforce the proposed controls effectively*; and

(6) the foreign policy consequences of not imposing controls.

Notwithstanding this congressional mandate, it appears that, to date, consideration of proposed foreign policy export controls on the basis of the foregoing criteria has been the exception rather than the rule. Thus, for example, with respect to the U.S. embargo on the export and re-export of oil and gas equipment and technology to the Soviet Union, (i) the equipment and technology were readily available from other sources (albeit licensees of U.S. technical data); (ii) the reaction of the Western European nations was, at best, uncooperative, and, indeed, hostile; (iii) enforcement efforts, at least against European suppliers supported by their own governments, were unsuccessful; and (iv) U.S. suppliers were forced to abandon supply contracts, with a corresponding loss of export income and jobs to the United States. It can, therefore, be anticipated that the scope of the president's power to impose export controls for foreign policy purposes will be a critical issue in congressional consideration of the extension of the Export Administration Act this year.

At the present time, the following foreign-policy-related export controls are in force:

(1) An almost complete embargo is in effect with respect to the export of any goods or technical data to Cuba, North Korea, Vietnam, and Kampuchea.[39]

(2) In response to the racial policies of the South African government, an embargo is in effect on the export to South Africa and/or Namibia of arms, military hardware, and equipment for the manufacture of military equipment, and certain commodities and technical data for which the exporter knows or has reason to know that the

commodities or technical data will be sold to, or used by, military or police entities in South Africa, or will be used to implement the policy of *apartheid*.[40]

(3) In response to evidence showing official support for international terrorism, a general prohibition (subject to exception on a case-by-case basis) on the export to Syria or South Yemen of crime control and detection equipment, certain specified military vehicles and machinery to produce military equipment, and aircraft and helicopters.[41]

(4) Libya is also subject to the antiterrorism restrictions discussed in the preceding paragraph. In addition, a validated license is required for the export to Libya of essentially all commodities and technical data, except food and medical supplies.[42]

(5) Effective March 30, 1984, a validated license is required for the export to Iran and Iraq of certain chemicals that are used in the manufacture of poison gas. Validated license applications for such exports will be denied when there is evidence that the chemicals may be used to produce chemical weapons.[43]

Export Control Procedures by Company

The U.S. exporter is legally responsible for ensuring that the licensing and other requirements of the Export Administration Regulations have been satisfied for any commodities or technical data that the exporter proposes to sell abroad.[44] As a result, any U.S. firm that proposes to implement an international marketing program should first determine if any of the foregoing export controls are applicable to the commodities or technical data that it proposes to export. If the commodities or technical data are subject to export controls, an application for the appropriate validated license must be submitted to the Office of Export Administration of the Department of Commerce. Exporters should be aware of the fact that the processing of validated license applications for the export of controlled goods and technical data to noncommunist countries is likely to take at least three to four weeks. The processing of validated license applications for exports to communist countries may take considerably longer. Needless to say, applications for validated licenses to export goods or technical data, which are subject to embargo for foreign policy or strategic reasons, will be denied.

Although the Commerce Department's Office of Export Administration is the licensing authority under the export control program, it is actually the Customs Service that is responsible for monitoring compliance with the regulations, in the sense of ensuring that each export of commodities and technical data from the United States is properly licensed at the time of shipment. In this context, the principal export control document is the Shipper's Export Declaration. At the time commodities to be exported are delivered to the carrier, the exporter or its freight forwarder must present a Shipper's Export Declaration to the carrier, indicating the type (i.e., general or validated) and number of the export license under which the goods are shipped. The carrier then files the Shipper's Export Declaration with the Customs Service, which confirms that the shipment is authorized pursuant to a general or a validated license, and that the commercial documents (invoice, bill of lading, packing lists, etc.) conform to the Shipper's Export Declaration and the exporter's validated license, if required.[45] Goods that have not been properly authorized for export may be seized by the Customs Service.[46]

Penalties for Noncompliance

The importance of compliance with the licensing provisions and other requirements of the Export Administration Regulations cannot be overemphasized. The Export Administration Act and Regulations provide that violators of these export control provisions are subject to any or *all* of the following sanctions:[47] criminal penalties, of fines of $50,000 or five times the value of the exported goods and/or imprisonment for up to five years;[48] civil penalties of $10,000 per violation; and administrative sanctions, including the suspension or revocation of outstanding validated licenses, the denial of pending and future validated license applications, and/or the suspension or denial of export privileges.

There is growing concern among government officials that a substantial volume of U.S. goods and technical data have been exported without proper licenses and in violation of U.S. export controls. The Intelligence Community's Report on Soviet Acquisition of Western Technology, issued in April 1982, states that, by means of unlicensed exports and diversion of licensed exports from their intended destinations, as well as through covert activities, the Soviet Union has acquired millions of dollars worth of Western high-technology equipment and technical data with direct military or strategic applications. As a result, Commerce and Justice Department officials have recently reaffirmed their intention to step up enforcement activities and to seek much more severe penalties for violations of these export controls.

U.S. firms that intend to implement international marketing programs should establish formal export control compliance programs to ensure that they will not run afoul of the Export Administration Regulations.

U.S. ANTIBOYCOTT REGULATIONS

As part of the continuing controversy between Israel and the Arab nations, the member states of the Arab League maintain an economic boycott of Israel. In an attempt to weaken Israel's economic and military power, Bahrain, Iraq, Jordan, Kuwait, Lebanon, Libya, Oman, Qatar, Saudi Arabia, Syria, the United Arab Emirates, the Yemen Arab Republic, and the People's Democratic Republic of Yemen restrict trade between themselves and Israel.[49] Moreover, in some instances, these nations impose restrictions on the extent to which their trading partners may also trade with Israel or with third parties that have ties with Israel. U.S. firms that propose to do business with or in Arab countries may encounter boycott requirements in a variety of contexts, such as: (a) the requirement that a response to a standard boycott questionnaire, regarding business ties with Israel, be submitted to the local government authorities in connection with (i) the appointment of a local distributor or commercial agent,[50] (ii) the registration of a trademark, (iii) the qualification of a local branch office, or (iv) the incorporation of a local subsidiary; (b) the requirement that the United States firm provide boycott-related information, or make a boycott-related certification, in connection with a tender on an Arab government contract or request for proposal; (c) boycott-related undertakings included in proposed contracts with both public sector and private sector entities in Arab countries;[51] (d) boycott-related certification requirements included in letters of credit opened by Arab customers in payment for goods purchased from U.S. suppliers;[52] and (e) requests for information regarding the nationality, national origin, and religion of employees that are to be sent to perform in-country services under a contract with an Arab customer.

In response to Arab pressures on U.S. firms to comply with the boycott of Israel and, on occasion, to honor the Arab blacklist of firms that are deemed to support Israel, the United States has established *two separate programs* of antiboycott regulations.[53] Section 999 of the Internal Revenue Code, enacted as part of the Tax Reform Act of 1976, provides for the imposition of income tax penalties on U.S. taxpayers that agree, as a condition of doing business with or in an Arab country, or with a national of an Arab country, to participate in or cooperate with the boycott of Israel. Section 8 of the Export Administration Act,[54] originally enacted as part of the Export Administration Amendments of 1977, specifically prohibits U.S. persons and firms from taking or agreeing to take certain specified boycott-related actions, in connection with any transaction in U.S. commerce, with intent to comply with, foster, or support the boycott of Israel. The single most important point to be stressed about these two programs of antiboycott regulation is that they are *inconsistent* as to their respective jurisdictional scopes, substantive prohibitions, reporting requirements, and penalties. Thus, because the antiboycott provisions of the Export Administration Act are limited to transactions involving U.S. persons *and* in U.S. commerce, transactions between a foreign affiliate of a U.S. firm and an Arab customer may be *outside* the jurisdictional scope of the Export Administration Act. Such transactions would, however, be *within* the jurisdictional scope of § 999 of the Internal Revenue Code. In contrast, because the penalties provided for in § 999 of the Internal Revenue Code apply only in the event of an *agreement* to participate in or comply with the boycott, various forms of boycott-related conduct, such as responding to a boycott questionnaire, may be outside the substantive provisions of § 999, but would be specifically prohibited by the substantive antiboycott provisions of the Export Administration Act.

Internal Revenue Code § 999

As noted above, § 999 of the Internal Revenue Code provides for the imposition of income tax penalties where a U.S. taxpayer, or a foreign affiliate of a U.S. taxpayer, agrees, as a condition of doing business with or in an Arab country, or with a national or company of an Arab country, to participate in or cooperate with the boycott of Israel. Section 999 was enacted as part of the Tax Reform Act of 1976,[55] in response to the failure of Congress to enact comprehensive federal antiboycott legislation. Such comprehensive antiboycott legislation was ultimately enacted in 1977 as part of the Export Administration Act,[56] and, as a result, there have been repeated proposals to repeal § 999. The proponents of this antiboycott tax legislation have, however, successfully resisted repeal efforts on the ground that § 999 of the Internal Revenue Code covers boycott-related conduct by foreign affiliates of U.S. firms which may be beyond the jurisdictional scope of the antiboycott provisions of the Export Administration Act. At this point, the chances of repeal of § 999 in the foreseeable future appear slim.

Jurisdictional Scope

Section 999(b) provides for the imposition of antiboycott tax penalties where a U.S. taxpayer, or any member of a controlled group that includes the taxpayer, agrees to participate in or cooperate with the boycott. For purposes of this section, a controlled group of corporations includes all corporations, foreign or domestic, in which more than 50 percent of the equity is owned, directly or indirectly, by the same interests.[57] Thus, the antiboycott provisions of the Internal Revenue Code are clearly applicable to boycott-related conduct of foreign subsidiaries of U.S. firms, *even if such conduct is undertaken in connection with transactions that have no nexus with the United States.* It is this broad jurisdictional reach of § 999 that has created considerable difficulties for U.S. firms that have assigned responsibility for Arab markets to their European subsidiaries.

The Concept of an "Agreement" to Participate in
or Cooperate with the Boycott

A taxpayer will be subject to antiboycott tax penalties only if it *agrees*, as a condition of doing business with Arab customers, to participate in or cooperate with the boycott. The concept of "agreement to participate in, or cooperate with," the boycott is defined in § 999 (b)(3) to include any agreement:

 (i)   to refrain from doing business with Israel or with Israeli nationals or firms;
 (ii) to refrain from doing business with a U.S. person or firm that has been blacklisted by the Arabs because of his/her or its ties with Israel;
 (iii) to refrain from doing business with any company because of the nationality, race, or religion of its owners or management;
 (iv) to refrain from employing individuals on the basis of their nationality, race, or religion; or
 (v)   to refrain from shipping goods on a blacklisted carrier or insuring goods with a blacklisted insurance company.

Examples of specific contexts in which a taxpayer will be deemed to have agreed to participate in or cooperate with the boycott are identified in extensive guidelines published by the Treasury Department.[58] Of particular importance to U.S. exporters is the fact that the guidelines indicate that boycott-related terms of a letter of credit opened in favor of a U.S. firm, in payment for goods exported to an Arab customer, will be deemed to be part of the U.S. firm's agreement with its customer, and therefore within the purview of § 999.[59]

Penalties

In the case that a taxpayer, or an affiliate of the taxpayer, has agreed to participate in or cooperate with the boycott, the following penalties may be applicable: (i) the loss of tax credits for foreign taxes paid on boycott-related income;[60] (ii) the loss of deferral of U.S. taxation of boycott-related income earned by a controlled foreign subsidiary of the taxpayer;[61] (iii) the loss of deferral of taxation of boycott-related income earned by the taxpayer on export sales conducted through a Domestic International Sales Corporation (DISC.)[62]

It should be emphasized that participation in or cooperation with the boycott in one transaction may lead to the imposition of tax penalties with respect to all income earned by the taxpayer and its affiliates from transactions with or in boycotting countries. Under § 999(b)(1) of the Internal Revenue Code, boycott participation in one transaction with an Arab country will taint all other transactions with that country and with all other Arab countries that are parties to the boycott, unless the taxpayer can show that its other transactions are clearly separate and distinguishable from the boycott-related transaction and do not involve boycott-related conduct.

Reporting Requirements

In order to monitor compliance with the substantive provisions of § 999, § 999(a)(1) provides that if a taxpayer, or a controlled group that includes the taxpayer, has operations with or in any boycotting country, the taxpayer must file a report of such operations with the Internal Revenue Service.[63] The report, IRS form 5713, is filed at the time the taxpayer files its annual income tax return. It should be emphasized that form 5713 must be filed if the taxpayer has any operations with or in a boycotting country, even if none of those operations involves participation in or cooperation with the boycott.[64]

Export Administration Act

As noted above, § 8 of the Export Administration Act[65] prohibits U.S. persons from taking, or agreeing to take, certain specified actions in connection with any transaction in U.S. commerce with intent[66] to comply with, foster, or support the boycott. This statute is intended to create a comprehensive program of regulation of boycott-related conduct, and violators may be subject to severe criminal, civil, and administrative penalties.

Jurisdictional Scope

The antiboycott provisions of the Export Administration Act apply only to boycott-related actions taken by U.S. persons in connection with transactions in U.S. commerce. Unless *both* of these jurisdictional requirements are satisfied, boycott-related conduct is not subject to the provisions of the Act.

The regulations implementing the Act[67] define the term "U.S. person" broadly to include not only U.S. citizens and residents and U.S. corporations, but also foreign branches, subsidiaries, and "controlled in fact" affiliates of U.S. firms.[68] Under this definition, foreign wholly or majority-owned subsidiaries of U.S. corporations will almost always be deemed "U.S. persons," and even minority-owned foreign affiliates may be deemed "U.S. persons" in the case that the U.S. shareholder is in a position to exercise effective control over the foreign firm (e.g., by virtue of ownership of a controlling equity interest, a management contract, or the power to appoint a majority of the board of directors).

Even if a particular firm is a U.S. person within the meaning of the Act, its boycott-related conduct will not be subject to the substantive antiboycott provisions of the Act unless such conduct is undertaken in connection with a transaction in U.S. commerce. Exports of goods and services from the United States and imports of goods and services into the United States will invariably be transactions in U.S. commerce.[69] More difficult interpretive problems with respect to the concept of U.S. commerce arise, however, where boycott-related actions are undertaken by foreign affiliates of U.S. firms. The regulations define the concept of "U.S. commerce" broadly, so that a sale of goods or services by a foreign affiliate of a U.S. firm to an Arab customer will generally be deemed to be a transaction in U.S. commerce, in the case that the goods or services were acquired from a person in the United States or incorporate components, materials, or services were acquired from a person in the United States *for the purpose of filling particular orders*.[70] In contrast, the sale of goods or services that are entirely of foreign origin will be deemed to be outside the scope of U.S. commerce for purposes of the antiboycott provisions of the Export Administration Act.[71]

Prohibited Boycott-Related Conduct

Assuming the jurisdictional prerequisites of the Act are satisfied, the following types of boycott-related conduct (and agreements to take such conduct) are prohibited:

(i) refusing or requiring another person or firm to refuse to do business with Israel, with Israeli nationals and firms, or with blacklisted firms;

(ii) refusing or requiring another person to refuse to hire a U.S. person on the basis of race, religion, sex, or national origin;[72]

(iii) furnishing information about the race, religion, sex, or national origin of a U.S. person;

(iv) furnishing information about any person's business relations with Israel, with Israeli nationals and firms, or with blacklisted firms;

(v) furnishing information about any person's membership in, or support of, a charitable or fraternal organization that supports Israel; and

(vi) implementing a letter of credit that requires the beneficiary to take prohibited boycott action or provide prohibited boycott-related information.

Examples of the forms of conduct that are within the scope of these prohibitions are given in extensive regulations published by the Department of Commerce, which administers the Export Administration Act.[73] Of particular concern to U.S. firms that propose to do business in Arab countries, or that seek to export their products to Arab countries, is the prohibition on furnishing information about business relationships with Israel and with blacklisted firms. Many Arab countries require U.S. firms to respond to a questionnaire about their activities in Israel in order to bid on government contracts or to organize a local branch or subsidiary. Letters of credit opened by Arab customers in payment for goods purchased from U.S. suppliers are frequently payable only upon presentation of boycott certifications. The most frequently encountered Arab boycott certification and information requirements are analyzed under the antiboycott provisions of the Export Administration Act, as well as under § 999 of the Internal Revenue Code, in Table 5.2. As the table shows, compliance with many of the most common requests for information or certifications is prohibited.

Penalties

Violators of the antiboycott provisions of the Export Administration Act may be subject to any or all of the following penalties:[74] (i) crim-

Table 5.2 Requests for Boycott-Related Action under U.S. Antiboycott Regulations

Requested Boycott Action	Export Administration Regulations[a]		IRC § 999d
	Reporting Regulations[b]	Substantive Regulations[c]	
1. Provision of a positive certificate of origin	not reportable	permitted	permitted
2. Provision of a negative certificate of origin	reportable	prohibited after June 21, 1978	permitted
3. Provision of a "war risk" certificate of origin	not reportable	permitted	permitted
4. Provision of a "war risk" certificate re: vessel owned by, or chartered to, an Israeli person or firm	not reportable	permitted	permitted
5. Provision of a "war risk" certificate re: vessel not scheduled to call at Israeli port prior to arrival at port of destination	not reportable	permitted	permitted
6. Provision of a "no blacklisted vessel" certificate	reportable	prohibited after June 21, 1978	prohibited
7. Provision of a "no blacklisted supplier" certificate (self-certification)	reportable	permitted	prohibited
8. Provision of a "no blacklisted supplier" certificate (certification as to third parties)	reportable	prohibited after June 21, 1978	prohibited
9. Provision of "vessel eligible" certificate (Egypt, Saudi Arabia)	not reportable	permitted	permitted
10. Provision of "vessel eligible" certificate, to be made by the exporter (countries other than Egypt and Saudi Arabia)	reportable	prohibited	prohibited
11. Provision of "vessel eligible" certificate, to be made by the vessel owner	not reportable after July 1, 1982	permitted	prohibited
12. Provision of "insurer's resident agent" certificate (Egypt and Saudi Arabia)	not reportable	permitted	permitted

(Table 5.2 continues)

79

Table 5.2 continued

Requested Boycott Action	Export Administration Regulations[a]		IRC § 999[d]
	Reporting Regulations[b]	Substantive Regulations[c]	
13. Provision of "insurer's resident agent" certificate, to be made by the exporter (countries other than Egypt and Saudi Arabia)	reportable	prohibited	prohibited
14. Provision of "insurer's resident agent" certificate, to be made by the insurer	not reportable after July 1, 1982	permitted	prohibited
15. Certification as to identity of supplier, shipping company, insurance carrier, etc.	not reportable	permitted	permitted
16. Compliance with unilateral selection of supplier, shipping company, etc. by Arab customer	not reportable unless recipient knows or has reason to know that selection is boycott based	permitted (under limited circumstances)	permitted
17. Provision of "seven questions" information	reportable	prohibited (except by bona fide resident of boycotting country)	permitted unless furnished pursuant to a prior agreement
18. Agreement to comply with laws of boycotting country (stated generally)	not reportable	permitted	prohibited
19. Agreement to comply with boycotting country's boycott laws	reportable	prohibited	prohibited
20. Agreement not to do business with or in Israel	reportable	prohibited	prohibited
21. Agreement not to obtain goods covered by specific order from Israel or from an Israeli firm	reportable	permitted	permitted

80

22. Negotiation of a letter of credit prohibiting shipment of Israeli goods	permitted	permitted, provided no certification is made	reportable
23. Negotiation of a Saudi letter of credit prohibiting shipment of goods or packaging bearing any symbols prohibited in Saudi Arabia	permitted	permitted	not reportable
24. Negotiation of a letter of credit prohibiting shipment of goods or packaging bearing a six-pointed star	permitted	prohibited	reportable
25. Agreement not to do business with a blacklisted U.S. person or firm	prohibited	prohibited	reportable
26. Agreement not to obtain goods covered by a specific order from a blacklisted U.S. person	prohibited	prohibited	reportable
27. Agreement to "risk of loss" provision	permitted	permitted	not reportable[e]

[a] The analysis of the Commerce Department's Anti-Boycott Regulations set forth in this chart assumes that the boycott-related request is received by a "U.S. person" and that the request relates to a transaction within "the interstate and foreign commerce of the United States," so that jurisdictional prerequisites are satisfied.

[b] As indicated in the text, the *receipt* of a boycott request is the reportable event, regardless of how the recipient responds or intends to respond to the request.

[c] This column indicates legality or illegality of compliance with specific boycott requests under the substantive Commerce Department Anti-Boycott Regulations.

[d] Internal Revenue Code § 999 provides for the imposition of tax penalties in the case that a U.S. taxpayer, or its foreign affiliate, *agrees*, as a condition of doing business in an Arab country, to participate in or cooperate with the boycott of Israel. Certification requirements contained in a letter of credit issued in connection with a sales transaction are deemed to be additional terms of the sales contract. Thus, compliance with a prohibited boycott-related letter of credit certification requirement is deemed to constitute an agreement to participate in the boycott.

[e] The receipt, after July 1, 1982, of a request for agreement to a "risk of loss" provision is not reportable, provided the firm from which the request is received adopted a policy of requiring agreement to such provisions in its contracts or purchase orders prior to January 18, 1978.

inal: fines of up to $50,000, or in the case of an export transaction, five times the value of the exported goods, whichever is greater, and/or imprisonment for up to five years; (ii) civil: fines of up to $10,000 per violation; and (iii) administrative: revocation or suspension of outstanding validated export licenses or denial of export privileges with respect to some or all destinations.

The Commerce Department's Office of Anti-Boycott Compliance has pursued an aggressive enforcement policy. To date, between 60 and 70 firms have been subject to sanctions for violation of the antiboycott provisions of the Export Administration Act. In most of these cases, the sanctions imposed have been fines of from $500 to $10,000 (the statutory maximum) per violation, but in one recent case the export privileges of the firm in question were suspended, at least with respect to specified Arab countries.[75] The imposition of this latter sanction could mean disaster for a U.S. firm that earns a substantial portion of its revenue from export sales.

Reporting Requirements

In addition to prohibiting specified forms of boycott-related conduct, the Export Administration Act requires U.S. persons to file reports of *all requests* for boycott-related action received in connection with any transaction or prospective transaction in U.S. commerce.[76] It should be emphasized that the *receipt* by a U.S. person of any request to take boycott-related action, or to provide boycott-related information, is the event that "triggers" the obligation to file a boycott report with the Office of Anti-Boycott Compliance. Thus, a boycott report must be filed upon receiving a boycott request, even if the U.S. person or firm in question does not intend to comply with the request, and even if the requested boycott-related action is not prohibited by the substantive antiboycott provisions of the Act and its implementing regulations.[77] Reports may be filed on a transaction by transaction basis on form ITA-621P or on a quarterly basis on form ITA-6051P. The reportability of common Arab boycott requests is analyzed in Table 5.2.

It should be emphasized that when a letter of credit that is confirmed through a U.S. bank requires the beneficiary to make a boycott-related certification, both the beneficiary (i.e., the U.S. exporter) and the confirming bank must file boycott reports.[78] The Office of Anti-Boycott Compliance is currently using computer cross-checks to confirm that both the banks and the beneficiaries have reported boycott-related letter of credit certification requests. That agency is quick to investigate letter of credit transactions which have been reported by a bank but have not been reported by the letter of credit beneficiaries.

Compliance with U.S. programs of antiboycott regulation is a complex and often exasperating endeavor. The two separate programs are inconsistent, and the Treasury Department and the Commerce Department have, on a number of occasions, adopted conflicting interpretations with respect to a particular Arab boycott clause or requirement. Moreover, Arab boycott requirements change frequently, and a mere change in the wording of a particular clause, without changing its meaning, can convert a permissive clause into a prohibitive clause. Thus, for example, under the Export Administration Act, and its implementing regulations, a U.S. exporter may lawfully *agree* with its Arab customer that the goods to be exported will not be manufactured in Israel. After the fact, however, the same exporter may *not* lawfully certify to its Arab customer that the goods were not manufactured in Israel.[79]

Due to the complexities and inconsistencies in the area of antiboycott regulation, U.S. firms that propose to do business in, or market their products in, Arab countries should work with experienced counsel from the outset in formulating their business plans. Firms should establish antiboycott procedures to place marketing and export personnel on notice of the boycott problems that are likely to be encountered in doing business with or in Arab countries, and to provide general guidance as to the appropriate response to the most common Arab boycott requests. Major transactions and unusual boycott requirements should be carefully reviewed by experienced counsel to assure that compliance will not constitute a violation of either program of antiboycott regulation. The consequences of noncompliance are too severe to be ignored.

NOTES

1. 50 U.S.C. App. § § 2401-2420.

2. 15 C.F.R. § § 368.1 *et seq.*

3. Under authority of the Arms Export Control Act of 1976, as amended, 22 U.S.C. § § 2751-2794, the Office of Munitions Control of the Department of State regulates the export of munitions, military hardware, and technical data having direct military applications. The State Department's regulatory program is set forth in the International Traffic in Arms Regulations, 22 C.F.R. § § 121.01 *et seq.*

4. 50 U.S.C. App. § 2402(2)(A). *See, also, id.* § 2404 (national security controls).

5. 50 U.S.C. App. § 2402(2)(B). *See, also, id.* § 2405 (foreign policy controls).

6. 50 U.S.C. App. § 2402(2)(C). *See, also, id.* § 2406 (short supply controls).

7. The various types of export licenses are established under authority of 50 U.S.C. App. § 2403(a).

8. Export Administration Regulations, 15 C.F.R. §§ 371.1 *et seq.*

9. Export Administration Regulations, 15 C.F.R. §§ 372.1 *et seq.*

10. *See* Export Administration Regulations, 15 C.F.R. § 370.1.

11. Export Administration Regulations, 15 C.F.R. § 399.1, Supplement No. 1.

12. Export Administration Regulations, 15 C.F.R. §§ 373.2 *et seq.*

13. *Id.,* § 373.2.

14. *Id.,* § 373.3.

15. *See id.,* § 373.3(c)(1).

16. *See id.,* § 373.3(a). The analogous special licensing procedure for export of goods to communist countries is a *qualified general license.* Under § 373.4 of the Export Administration regulations, the Commerce Department may issue a qualified general license for the export of restricted commodities to approved end-users for approved end-uses in China (Country Group P), Romania (Country Group Q), Poland and Hungary (Country Group W), and the Soviet Union, Mongolia, and the balance of communist Eastern Europe (Country Group Y). *See* 15 C.F.R. § 373.4. To date, few, if any, qualified general licenses have been issued by the Commerce Department, and the Reagan Administration has proposed the elimination of the qualified general license procedure.

17. 49 Fed. Reg. 2264-67 (January 19, 1984).

18. Export Administration Regulations, 15 C.F.R. § 379.1(a).

19. *See* Export Administration Regulations, 15 C.F.R. § 379.1(b).

20. Export Administration Regulations, 15 C.F.R. § 379.3(a).

21. Export Administration Regulations, 15 C.F.R. § 379.4. The technical data for which written assurances against diversion are required are identified in § 379.4(f)(1)(i)(a)-(g).

22. *See* 48 Fed. Reg. 25171 (June 6, 1983), *amending,* 15 C.F.R. § 379.4(g). In addition, the June 6, 1983 amendments provide that a validated license is required for any export of (i) software listed on the Commodity Control List (e.g., software for machinery for the manufacture of electronic equipment, ECCN 1355 [A]); and (ii) all applications software relating to items identified in §§ 379.4(c) and (d) of the regulations.

23. Validated licenses are required for the export to any destination of technical data relating to the items specified in § 379.4(c) (e.g., information for the design and production of nuclear weapons or nuclear materials). Validated licenses are required for the export to any destination *except Canada* of technical data relating to the items specified in § 379.4(d) (e.g., information relating to navigation and guidance systems for aircraft).

24. Similarly, the general license GTDR may not be used in connection with any technical data export to Libya or to the embargoed destinations, Cuba, Kampuchea, North Korea, and Vietnam. *See* 15 C.F.R. § 379.4(a).

25. Export Administration Regulations, 15 C.F.R. § 379.4(b)(1)(i)-(v). Under limited circumstances technical data supporting a bid or quotation may be exported to a communist country under general license GTDR, provided that the technical data do not disclose the design, production, or manufacture of the quoted commodity. *See* 15 C.F.R. § 379.4(b)(2).

26. Under § 376.10(a)(1)(vii) of the regulations, an application for a validated license to export digital computers to a restricted destination (i.e., a communist country) must include a detailed description of all software that will be exported for use with the computer.

27. *See id.,* § § 374.1, 379.8(a).

28. *See id.,* § 385.2(c)(1). The restrictions extend to any person subject to the jurisdiction of the United States. The term "person subject to the jurisdiction of the United States" includes any firm, wherever located or incorporated, which is owned or controlled by one or more U.S. citizens or residents or by a U.S. corporation. *See id.,* § 385.2(c)(2)(iv). The restrictions on the export of oil and gas equipment and technical data to the Soviet Union were lifted on November 13, 1982. *See* 47 Fed. Reg. 51858-61 (November 18, 1982).

29. *See* Export Administration Regulations 15 C.F.R. § 374.3(a), (b).

30. *Id.,* § 385.4(b)(1)(ii).

31. Validated licenses are required for virtually all exports to the embargoed countries, Cuba, Kampuchea, North Korea, and Vietnam. Applications for validated licenses to export to those countries will be summarily denied. *See* Export Administration Regulations, 15 C.F.R. § 385.1.

32. *See id.,* § 385.2(a)(1).

33. On December 29, 1981, the Office of Export Administration adopted a policy of approving validated license applications for the export to China of high-tech items having technical levels approximately twice as high as previously authorized for export to communist countries. *See* 46 Fed. Reg. 62836 (December 29, 1981).

34. 48 Fed. Reg. 53064-71 (November 23, 1983).

35. *See* Export Administration Regulations, 15 C.F.R. § 370.13(1).

36. If COCOM approval is not granted within 60 days of the date of tentative U.S. government approval of a validated license application, the license will be granted unless the Office of Export Administration determines that issuance of the license without COCOM approval would be contrary to U.S. national security considerations.

37. *See, generally,* congressional findings, *codified as* 50 U.S.C. App. § 2402-(2).

38. 50 U.S.C. App. § 2405(b).

39. Export Administration Regulations, 15 C.F.R. § 385.1.

40. *Id.,* § 385.4(a), *as modified in* 47 Fed. Reg. 9201-06 (March 4, 1982), and 47 Fed. Reg. 40538-40 (September 15, 1982).

41. Export Administration Regulations, 15 C.F.R. § 385.4(d). Iraq was deleted from the list of countries that are subject to antiterrorism controls on March 1, 1982. At that time, antiterrorism controls were also relaxed on the sale of civil aircraft and helicopters to scheduled commercial airlines in Syria and South Yemen. *See* 47 Fed. Reg. 2901-06 (March 4, 1982). Pursuant to the specific mandate of Congress in the Export Administration Act, the export of crime control and detection equipment to all countries, other than the members of NATO, Japan, Australia, and New Zealand, is subject to review on a case-by-case basis. *See* 50 U.S.C. App. § 2405(j); 15 C.F.R. § 385.4(b)(2).

42. *See* 47 Fed. Reg. 11247 (March 16, 1982), *codified as* 15 C.F.R. § 385.7.

43. *See* 49 Fed. Reg. 13135-36 (April 3, 1984), *amending* 15 C.F.R. § 385.4.

44. Under § 387.4 of the regulations, even U.S. manufacturers that sell their products abroad solely through domestic trading companies have at least some duty to ensure that their goods will not be exported in violation of the Export Administration Regulations. Section 387.4 provides, *inter alia*, that no person may sell any commodity or technical data to be exported from the United States *with knowledge or reason to know* that the commodity or technical data will be exported in violation of the regulation or any license or order thereunder. *See* 15 C.F.R. § 387.4.

45. *See, generally,* Export Administration Regulations, 15 C.F.R. § § 386.1 *et seq.*

46. *See* 22 U.S.C. § 401; Export Administration Regulations, 15 C.F.R. § § 386.8(b)(6), 387.1(b)(4).

47. *See* 50 U.S.C. App. § 2410. *See, also,* 15 C.F.R. § 387.1.

48. Any firm that willfully exports goods or technical data in violation of the Export Administration Regulations with the knowledge that such goods or technical data will be used in a manner contrary to the national security or foreign policy export controls is punishable for each such violation by fines of $1 million or five times the value of the exports. *See* 50 U.S.C. App. § 2410(b)(1)(A). Individual violators are punishable by fines of up to $250,000 or five times the value of the exports and up to ten years imprisonment. *See id*. § 2410(b)(1)(B).

49. Prior to January 1, 1980, Egypt was also a party to the boycott of Israel. Egyptian boycott requirements have, however, been dropped as a result of the Egyptian-Israeli Peace Treaty.

50. Under Saudi Ministerial Decision No. 1897, all commercial agency and distributorship agreements between Saudi agents and foreign suppliers must be registered with the Saudi Ministry of Commerce. The Ministry of Commerce requires Saudi agents to make the following boycott-related certification on behalf of their foreign principals as part of that registration process:

I, the undersigned, hereby undertake in my capacity as _____ that [foreign principal] is not presently on the blacklist of Israel and that it and all of its branches, if any, adhere to decisions issued by the boycott office, and do not: (i) participate in the capital of, (ii) license the manufacture of any products or grant trademark or trade name licenses to, (iii) give experience or technical advice to, or (iv) have any other relationship with other companies which are prohibited to be dealt with by the boycott office.

51. The following boycott-related clause is frequently encountered in Saudi contracts:

In connection with the performance of this contract, the Supplier acknowledges that the import and customs laws and regulations of the Kingdom of Saudi Arabia shall apply to the furnishing and shipment of any products or components thereof to Saudi Arabia. The Supplier specifically asknowledges that the aforementioned import and customs laws and regulations of the Kingdom of Saudi Arabia prohibit, among other things, the importation into Saudi Arabia of products or components thereof: (1) originating in Israel, (2) manufactured, produced, or furnished by companies organized under the laws of Israel, and (3) manufactured, produced, or furnished by nationals or residents of Israel.

52. The point is illustrated by the following Bahrain boycott certification requirements attached to a letter of credit recently issued by the British Bank of the Middle East in Bahrain:

1. A certificate to the effect that the goods are not of Israeli origin and contain no Israeli labor or materials, and are not being exported from Israel.

2. A certificate to the effect that the vessel carrying the goods is eligible to enter the ports of Bahrain. Such a certificate by the vessel owner or master is acceptable.

53. Although the U.S. antiboycott legislation was enacted in response to the Arab boycott of Israel, both programs of antiboycott regulation are of general applicability, and may therefore restrict compliance with international boycotts other than the Arab boycott of Israel. Boycott requirements in connection with non-Arab countries may be encountered in connection with transactions with Nigeria (directed at South Africa and, on occasion, Israel), Pakistan (directed at Israel, South Africa, Taiwan, and, on occasion, India), and the People's Republic of China (directed at Taiwan).

54. 50 U.S.C. App. § 2407.

55. Public Law 94-455, 90 Stat. 1649.

56. 50 U.S.C. App. § 2407, originally enacted as § 201 of the Export Administration Amendments of 1977, Public Law 95-52, 91 Stat. 244.

57. *See* IRC § 993(a)(3).

58. Tax Reform Act of 1976 Guidelines: International Boycotts, 1978-1 Cum. Bull. 521-49, *as amended by* 1979-2 Cum. Bull. 495-97.

59. *See* Guidelines H-8, 1978-1 Cum. Bull. 537.

60. *See* IRC § 908(a).

61. *See* IRC § 952(a)(3)(B).

62. *See* IRC § 995(b)(1)(F)(ii).

63. The details of this reporting requirement are set forth in § A of the guidelines, 1978-1 Cum. Bull. 521-28.

64. *See, e.g.,* Guideline A-9, 1978-1 Cum. Bull. 523.

65. 50 U.S.C. App. § 2407.

66. To satisfy the *intent* requirement it is sufficient that the U.S. firm intended to take the action it took (e.g., entering into a contract containing boycott undertakings; making a boycott-related letter of credit certification; answering a boycott questionnaire). There is no need for the government to show, in an enforcement proceeding, that the firm in question actually desired to assist the Arabs in their conflict with Israel. *See* Export Administration Regulations, 15 C.F.R. § 369.1(e)(4).

67. Export Administration Regulations, 15 C.F.R. §§ 369.1 *et seq.*

68. *See, generally*, 15 C.F.R. §§ 369.1(b), 369.1(c).

69. 15 C.F.R. § 369.1(d)(2).

70. 15 C.F.R. § 369.1(d)(8).

71. 15 C.F.R. § 369.1(d)(11).

72. As with IRC § 999, only discriminatory action that is taken in response to a *boycott request* is within the purview of the antiboycott provisions of the Export Administration Act. Although certain Arab countries may require their U.S. contractors to exclude women from consideration for certain in-country positions, based on local customs and traditions, compliance with such discriminatory requirements would not violate the antiboycott provisions of the Export Administration Act. Such discrimination on the basis of sex might, however, violate other

provisions of law, such as Title VII of the 1964 Civil Rights Act, *as amended*, 42 U.S.C. § 2000e.

73. Export Administration Regulations, 15 C.F.R. § § 369.1 *et seq.*

74. *See* 50 U.S.C. App. § 2410; 15 C.F.R. § 387.1.

75. To date, no criminal penalties have been imposed for violation of the antiboycott provisions of the Act.

76. *See* 50 U.S.C. App. § 2407(b)(2); 15 C.F.R. § 369.6.

77. *See* 15 C.F.R. § 369.6(a)(1).

78. *See* 15 C.F.R. § 369.6 example (xx).

79. Table 5.2 identifies some of the inconsistencies between the Export Administration Act and § 999 of the Internal Revenue Code, and some of the complexities that are likely to be encountered in this area. The table is for general guidance only, and because slight differences in wording or particular boycott clauses can result in dramatic differences in consequences, actual boycott requests should be interpreted on the basis of consultation with experienced counsel.

6

SPECIAL TAX AND
LEGAL OPPORTUNITIES

THE DOMESTIC INTERNATIONAL SALES CORPORATION

The Internal Revenue Code, § § 991-97, provides for a system of tax deferral for a corporation known as a Domestic International Sales Corporation (or "DISC") and its shareholders. Under this regime DISC profits are not taxed to the DISC but are taxed to its shareholders when distributed or deemed distributed to them. Each year a DISC is deemed to have distributed a portion of its income, as discussed below, thereby subjecting that income to current taxation in the hands of the shareholders. Tax can generally be deferred on the remaining portion of the DISC income ("accumulated DISC income") until such income is actually distributed, a shareholder disposes of the DISC stock, the DISC is liquidated or sold, the corporation ceases to qualify as a DISC, or a DISC election is terminated or revoked.

In a typical case a DISC is a wholly owned subsidiary of a U.S. exporter. Thus, distributions and deemed distributions from the DISC are subject to corporate tax and, eventually, to tax at the shareholder level when such income is distributed. Many closely held exporting companies, however, have organized parallel or "sister" DISCs owned directly by the shareholders of the exporter. Under this structure income allocated to the DISC permanently escapes tax at the U.S. corporate 46 percent level, since DISC dividends flow directly to the individual shareholders. The DISC thus acts as a conduit for dividends from the exporter on a tax deductible basis.[1]

Qualification of DISC

To qualify for DISC deferral benefits, a DISC must be incorporated under the laws of a U.S. state or the District of Columbia, have single class of stock with an outstanding par stated value of at least $2,500, elect to be treated as a DISC, and satisfy the gross receipts and gross assets tests.

The gross receipts test requires that at least 95 percent of the corporation's gross receipts consist of qualified export receipts. Such receipts, including commission receipts, are generally derived from the sale or lease for use outside the United States of "export property," or from the furnishing of services related or subsidiary to the sale or lease of such export property. The gross assets test requires that at least 95 percent of the DISC's assets qualify as export assets. Qualified export assets include inventory of export property; necessary operational equipment and supplies; trade receivables from export sales; loans to U.S. producers (including a DISC's related parent or sister exporting company); working capital; obligations of domestic corporations organized solely to finance export sales under guarantee agreements with the Export-Import Bank; and obligations issued, guaranteed, or insured by the Export-Import Bank or the Foreign Credit Insurance Association.

A DISC's taxable year need not conform to the taxable year of any of its shareholders. Frequently a subsidiary or sister DISC has a taxable year ending one month after its major shareholder's taxable year. The DISC's deemed dividend is received by such major shareholder in its (or his/her) succeeding taxable year, thereby maximizing the deferral benefit.

If a DISC fails to meet the above qualifications for any reason, the Code provides for gradual recapture of DISC deferred income. Such recapture of deferred or accumulated DISC earnings is spread over a period equal to two years for each year the DISC was in existence up to a maximum of ten years.

Qualifying Income

DISC benefits are accorded to income from: (i) the sale or lease for use outside the United States of "export property" (defined below); (ii) services related or subsidiary to such sale of export property; (iii) certain engineering and architectural services for foreign construction projects; (iv) certain managerial services; (v) interest on any obligation which is a qualified export asset; (vi) certain qualifying dividends; and (vii) the sale of export assets.

"Export property" generally includes property manufactured, produced, grown, or extracted in the United States[2] and held for sale or lease to any person for use, consumption, or disposition outside the United States. DISC benefits are *not* allowed for: (i) property leased by a DISC to a member of a related group; (ii) patents or intangibles; (iii) property the sale of which is subsidized by the U.S. government; (iv) property in short supply; or (v) oil, gas, coal, or other depletable minerals. DISC benefits on the sale of military goods is half the amount otherwise allowed.

Income Earned by a DISC

A portion of a U.S. exporter's total export profit can be allocated to the tax-free DISC under special rules set forth in § 994 of the Code. Under the "safe harbor" rules up to 50 percent of the total export profit on the transaction, or 4 percent of gross receipts from such export transaction, may be "earned" by the DISC. A DISC need not perform any services for such income; i.e., it may serve simply as an incorporated bank account. The DISC, moreover, may receive an additional allocation of income equal to 10 percent of its export promotional expenses. Alternatively, the DISC may conduct an export business through its own employees and deal at arm's length with its related U.S. supplier under the rules set forth at Code Section 482.

Income Retained by a DISC and Tax Deferred

Of the income earned by a DISC, 57.5 percent is "deemed distributed" to its corporate parent[3] on the last day of its fiscal year, while 42.5 percent is retained as "accumulated DISC income" and deferred from tax. Deferral is provided for both export profits and qualifying investment income. Federal income tax on such "accumulated DISC income" may be deferred indefinitely until the income is actually distributed or if there is a sale, disposition, liquidation, disqualification, or termination of the DISC.

Amount of Benefit

The amount of the DISC benefit depends upon the method used to allocate income to the DISC. If the safe harbor rules are used, deferral is generally provided with respect to 21.25 percent of the total export profit, resulting in a reduction of the current tax on total export profit from 46 percent to 36.2 percent.[4] If income is earned by the DISC on an arm's length basis, deferral is 42.5 percent of such earned income.

As a result of the 1976 Tax Act, incremental rules currently limit DISC tax deferral benefits to income attributable to a taxpayer's export receipts which exceed 67 percent of his average gross receipts in a prior four-year base period.[5] Therefore, U.S. exporters must steadily increase their export base if significant DISC benefits are to be retained. These incremental rules are waived for small DISCs with adjustable taxable income of $100,000 or less.

The use of a DISC as an export incentive vehicle must now be carefully reevaluated in light of the Tax Reform Act of 1984, signed by the president on July 18, 1984. Under this Act a new tax incentive vehicle, the Foreign Sales Corporation (FSC) will be available to U.S. exporters, effective January 1, 1985. At that time the DISC benefits will be severely curtailed for most taxpayers. A general overview of the FSC legislation is set forth in the following section.

FOREIGN SALES CORPORATION

Introduction

Effective January 1, 1985, the benefits of a Domestic International Sales Corporation were severely curtailed for most taxpayers. On that date the new Foreign Sales Corporation provisions of the Tax Reform Act of 1984 (Tax Act) became effective. These provisions are intended to make U.S. export incentive legislation compatible to the General Agreement on Tariffs and Trade (GATT) and are based on the GATT rule that a country need not tax income from economic processes occurring outside its territory.[6]

GENERAL COMPARISON OF FSC AND DISC

An FSC, like a DISC, is a sales company which is entitled to special U.S. tax benefits on its export income. Similar to a DISC, export sales may be made through an FSC on a buy-sell or commission basis.[7] Unlike a DISC, however, an FSC must be incorporated in a foreign jurisdiction.

The DISC provisions generally permit indefinite deferral of U.S. taxes on a portion of a DISC's income.[8] In contrast, a portion of an FSC's export income (foreign trade income) is permanently exempted from U.S. taxation. A DISC is not required to have any substance or perform any services in order to obtain its tax deferral benefit.[9] Except for a small FSC generating $5 million or less in export sales, an

FSC qualifies for its tax exemption only if it undertakes certain economic activities outside the United States.

FORMAL REQUIREMENTS FOR FSC STATUS

Similar to a DISC, it is not difficult to organize an FSC. An FSC simply must meet the following organizational requirements:[10]

1. be organized in a U.S. possession or a qualifying foreign country;[11]
2. have no more than 25 shareholders;[12]
3. not issue preferred stock;
4. maintain an office in a U.S. possession or a qualifying foreign country and keep records at that office;[13]
5. maintain sufficient records in the United States to meet the general record keeping requirements of § 6001 of the Code;
6. have at least one director who is not a resident of the United States;
7. not be a member of a controlled group of corporations which includes a DISC;[14]
8. have a taxable year which conforms to the taxable year of the shareholder having the highest percentage of voting power (principal shareholder);[15] and
9. file a timely election to be treated as an FSC.

Unlike a DISC, an FSC has no minimum capitalization requirement, and there is no qualified "export assets" or "gross receipts" test.[16]

An election to be treated as an FSC for any taxable year must be made during the 90-day period preceding the beginning of the taxable year.[17] The temporary treasury regulations, however, permit an FSC electing to be treated as an FSC for its first taxable year to make the election within 90 days after the beginning of such taxable year.[18] This special rule was necessary to prevent premature termination of existing DISCs prior to December 31, 1984. Although an FSC must use the same accounting period as its principal shareholder, an FSC need not delay electing FSC status in 1985 until the beginning of its principal shareholder's taxable year. The FSC, however, must then close its first 1985 taxable year and adopt its principal shareholder's accounting period on the first day that such period begins in 1985.[19]

INCOME ELIGIBLE FOR FSC BENEFITS

The tax benefit provided by the FSC legislation is an exemption from tax for a portion of the FSC's foreign trade income. Foreign trade income is the gross income of an FSC attributable to foreign trading gross receipts.[20] With the exception of investment income and carrying charges, the same types of receipts which qualify for DISC benefits generally give rise to foreign trading gross receipts.[21]

Foreign Trading Gross Receipts

Foreign trading gross receipts include receipts from the following types of transactions:[22]

1. the sale, exchange, or other disposition of "export property";
2. the lease or rental of "export property" for use outside the United States;
3. the performance of services that are "related and subsidiary" to the transactions described above at (1) and (2);
4. the performance of engineering or architectural services for construction projects located outside the United States; and
5. the performance of managerial services furthering the production of the income described at (1), (2), and (3) by an unrelated FSC or DISC, provided the FSC earns at least 50 percent of its gross receipts from activities producing foreign trading gross receipts.

Receipts from the following transactions, however, do not qualify for FSC benefits:[23]

1. the sale of property or services for ultimate use in the United States or for use by a U.S. instrumentality required to use such property or services;
2. transactions subsidized by the United States or an instrumentality thereof;
3. the sale of property or services to an affiliated FSC;
4. investments by the FSC, including carrying charges; and
5. one-half of the receipts from the sale or lease of military property.

FSC Export Property

Property which is export property for a DISC essentially is export property for an FSC.[24] Thus, property is export property if: it is manufactured, produced, grown, or extracted in the United States by a person other than an FSC; it is held primarily for sale, lease, or rental in the ordinary course of business, by or to an FSC, for direct use, consumption, or disposition outside the United States;[25] and no more than 50 percent of its fair market value is attributable to articles imported into the United States.[26]

Similar to the DISC rules, the FSC legislation excludes the following property from the definition of export property:[27] property leased or rented by an FSC to an affiliate; intangibles, such as patents, inventions, designs, and copyrights (other than films, tapes, records, or similar reproductions); oil or gas and primary products thereof (but not depletable products such as coal); certain products subject to export control restrictions relating to protection of the domestic economy; and property designated by the president as in "short supply" domestically. Since the definition of export property contained in the FSC legislation essentially is the same as that contained in the DISC rules, the uncertainty surrounding the treatment of computer software as export property will carry over to the FSC rules.

EXEMPT FOREIGN TRADE INCOME

Determination of Foreign Trade Income

Similar to determining a DISC's income, an FSC's foreign trade income can be determined by using safe harbor pricing rules (administrative pricing rules), or on an arm's length basis.[28] Under the administrative pricing rules, an FSC can earn foreign trade income in an amount equal to the greater of 23 percent of total pretax export profits (combined taxable income of the FSC and its related supplier), or 1.83 percent of the FSC's foreign trading gross receipts (up to a limit of 46 percent of total pretax export profits).[29] The 1.83 percent alternative is intended for exporters operating with export profit margins of less than 8 percent.[30] Alternatively, an FSC may determine its foreign trade income on the basis of actual transactions with third parties, or under any method permitted under § 482 of the Code covering transactions between related parties.

The secretary is authorized to promulgate regulations allowing the intercompany pricing rules to be applied on the basis of groups or transactions based on product lines or recognized industry or trade usages.[31] It is expected that these rules will closely parallel the grouping rules contained in the current DISC regulations.[32]

Determination of Exempt Foreign Trade Income

The amount of an FSC's foreign trade income which is exempt from U.S. taxation depends upon whether the FSC determines its income under the administrative pricing rules or on an arm's length basis. If an FSC determines its income under the administrative pricing rules, 15/23 and 16/23 of the income is exempt for corporate and noncorporate shareholders, respectively.[33] For a corporate shareholder, therefore, 15 percent of total pretax export profit generally is exempt from U.S. taxation. For a noncorporate shareholder 16 percent of total pretax export profit is exempt. This exemption effectively reduces the U.S. tax rate imposed on the total export profit of an FSC and a corporate shareholder from 46 percent to 39 percent [(100 percent - (23 percent × 15/23)) × 46 percent].

Alternatively, for companies with profit margins of less than 8 percent, the exemption for a corporate and noncorporate shareholder, respectively, is 1.19 percent (15/23 × 1.83 percent) and 1.27 percent (16/23 × 1.83 percent) of the FSC's foreign gross receipts. Because up to 46 percent of the total export profit may be paid to an FSC under the 1.83 percent method, the U.S. tax rate on total export profit may be as low as 32 percent [(100 percent - (46 percent × 15/23)) × 46 percent].

If an FSC determines its income on an arm's length basis, 30 percent and 32 percent of the FSC's foreign trade income is exempt for corporate and noncorporate shareholders, respectively.[34] If an FSC earns 100 percent of the total export profit, this exemption effectively reduces the U.S. tax rate imposed on the total export profit of an FSC and a corporate shareholder from 46 percent to 32 percent [(100 percent - 30 percent) × 46 percent]. This could result, for example, if the FSC had an independent sales organization and did not acquire products from a related party. However, if an FSC earns 50 percent of the total export profit the U.S. tax rate is reduced only to 39 percent [(100 percent - (30 percent × 50 percent)) × 46 percent]. Thus, the arm's length pricing rules only would offer an advantage over the administrative pricing rules where an FSC may earn more than 50 percent of the total export profit on an arm's length basis.

U.S. TAXATION OF FSC INCOME

Foreign Trade Income

For purposes of United States taxation an FSC's foreign trade income may conveniently be grouped into the following four categories: (1) exempt income under the administrative pricing rules; (2) nonexempt income under the administrative pricing rules; (3) exempt income under an arm's length pricing method; and (4) nonexempt income under an arm's length pricing method.

Safe Harbor Exempt Income

An FSC's exempt foreign trade income determined under the administrative pricing rules is treated as foreign source income "not effectively" connected with a U.S. trade or business.[35] Thus, the income is exempt from U.S. corporate taxation in the hands of an FSC.[36] Such income also is not subject to the rules of subpart F.[37]

An FSC's exempt foreign trade income is further exempt from U.S. taxation upon distribution to a U.S. corporate shareholder by permitting such shareholder a 100 percent dividends received deduction.[38] A U.S. individual or other noncorporate shareholder is not permitted such a deduction. Thus, the only significant U.S. tax advantage of an FSC to a U.S. noncorporate shareholder is the shelter from U.S. corporate taxation of 16/23, rather than 15/23, of an FSC's foreign trade income. A foreign corporation or nonresident alien also is subject to U.S. taxation upon distributions made by an FSC out of its exempt foreign trade income, since such distributions are treated as U.S. source income effectively connected with a U.S. trade or business.[39]

Safe Harbor Nonexempt Income

An FSC's nonexempt foreign trade income determined under the administrative pricing rules is treated as U.S. source income effectively connected with a U.S. trade or business.[40] Consequently, it is subject to current U.S. taxation at the regular corporate rates.[41] This nonexempt foreign trade income, however, is not subject to the rules of subpart F.[42]

To avoid double taxation with respect to a U.S. corporate shareholder, such shareholder is permitted a 100 percent dividends received deduction for distributions out of an FSC's nonexempt foreign trade income.[43] No similar deduction is permitted for a U.S. individual or other noncorporate shareholder, and any distribution to a foreign corporation or nonresident alien is treated as income effectively connected with a U.S. trade or business.[44] Thus, there are no benefits to a noncorporate shareholder or a foreign shareholder with respect to that income.

Arm's Length Exempt Income

An FSC's exempt foreign trade income resulting from an arm's length transaction is subject to the same U.S. tax treatment as an FSC's exempt foreign trade income determined under the administrative pricing rules.[45] Thus, such income is exempt from corporate taxation and from the rules of subpart F. Moreover, this income is further exempt from taxation upon distribution to U.S. corporate shareholders, but is subject to taxation upon distribution to U.S. noncorporate and foreign shareholders.

Arm's Length Nonexempt Income

The taxation of an FSC's nonexempt foreign trade income resulting from an arm's length transaction is determined in the same manner as for a foreign corporation which is not an FSC.[46] If an FSC should purchase export property from a parent or affiliate, therefore, such nonexempt foreign trade income generally would be passed through to the FSC's U.S. shareholders under the subpart F rules and, thus, would be subject to current U.S. taxation.

Investment Income

An FSC's investment income and carrying charges are subject to double taxation and, thus, an FSC should avoid earning such income. Such passive income is subject to current U.S. corporate taxation by treating it as foreign source income effectively connected with a U.S. trade or business.[47] A distribution of this income also is taxed to the FSC's corporate and noncorporate shareholders, since there is no dividends-received deduction.[48] In order to avoid a third level of taxation, however, an FSC's investment income and carrying charges are excluded from subpart F treatment.[49]

Other Nonforeign Trade Income

The other nonforeign trade income of an FSC is taxed in the same manner as income earned by a foreign corporation that is not an FSC.[50] Consequently, such income would be subject to U.S. effectively connected and subpart F rules. Nonforeign trade income, therefore, probably could be more effectively sheltered from U.S. taxation through the use of other entities.

CREDITABILITY OF FOREIGN TAXES

The FSC provisions are designed to discourage incorporation of an FSC in a jurisdiction which imposes foreign taxes on the FSC's foreign trade income or withholding taxes on distributions of such income. Consequently, the ability of an FSC and its shareholders to claim credits or deductions for foreign taxes paid with respect to an FSC's foreign trade income is severely curtailed.

First, except with respect to nonexempt income resulting from an arm's length transaction, an FSC is not allowed a credit or deduction for foreign taxes paid with respect to its foreign trade income,[51] and such income is subject to a separate foreign tax credit limitation.[52] Second, except with respect to nonexempt income resulting from an arm's length transaction, dividends declared by an FSC to its U.S. shareholders out of foreign trade income carry no creditable foreign taxes for the U.S. recipient,[53] and such dividends also are subject to a separate foreign tax credit limitation.[54] By virtue of these separate limitations, an FSC's foreign source foreign trade income generally cannot be used to increase the permissible credit of foreign taxes against U.S. taxes due by either the FSC or its shareholders.[55]

Finally, the FSC legislation provides a special rule governing the source of income (and thus the foreign tax credit limitation) from sales by a person related to an FSC upon which the FSC earns income. Under this rule the related person's foreign source income from export transactions involving the FSC may not exceed the amount which would be treated as foreign source income earned by that person if the analogous DISC income allocation rules were applied.[56] For this purpose, the DISC "50-50" income allocation rule is analogous to the FSC "23 percent" of total pretax export profits method, and the DISC "4 percent" of gross receipts rule is analogous to the FSC "1.83 percent" of foreign trading gross receipts method.[57]

The creditability of foreign taxes relating to an FSC's nonexempt foreign trade income resulting from an arm's length transaction, investment income, and other nonforeign trade income is determined in the same manner as for a foreign corporation which is not an FSC.

PLACE OF INCORPORATION

An FSC must be incorporated in a possession of the United States or in a "qualifying foreign country."[58] For this purpose a U.S. possession includes Guam, American Samoa, the U.S. Virgin Islands and the Northern Mariana Islands, but not Puerto Rico.[59] Qualifying foreign countries include: countries which have executed an exchange of information agreement with the United States equivalent to that required by the Caribbean Basin legislation in section 274(h)(6)(C) of the Code; and countries which have a tax treaty with the United

States certified by the Treasury as having adequate exchange of information provisions.[60]

It is essential that the country in which an FSC is incorporated impose no or a minimal tax on the FSC's foreign trade income without regard to treaty benefits.[61] As discussed above, no credits generally are allowed for foreign taxes paid with respect to an FSC's foreign trade income. Thus, an FSC which pays any foreign taxes will reduce the U.S. tax savings on export sales on a dollar for dollar basis.[62] Presently a zero foreign tax on foreign trade income can be achieved by incorporating an FSC in a U.S. possession, since the FSC legislation prohibits any possession from taxing an FSC's foreign trade income derived before January 1, 1987.[63] In addition, a number of foreign countries are considering special legislation to reduce the tax on an FSC's foreign trade income to zero.[64]

REQUIRED FSC ACTIVITIES

Unlike a DISC, an FSC (with the exception of a "small FSC")[65] is entitled to the described tax benefits only if it performs certain managerial activities and economic processes outside the United States. These "foreign presence" requirements are designed to ensure that the FSC's exempt income arises from foreign economic activities in accordance with GATT principles. With the exception of certain binding agreements executed prior to 1985, no costs incurred or activities performed prior to January 1, 1985 are taken into account for purposes of satisfying these requirements.[66]

The management of an FSC must take place outside the United States.[67] Management of an FSC is treated as occurring outside the United States if the FSC: (1) holds all meetings of its board of directors and shareholders outside the United States; (2) maintains its principal bank account outside the United States at all times during the taxable year; and (3) makes all disbursements of dividends, legal and accounting fees, officers' salaries and directors' fees from bank accounts maintained outside the United States.[68] An FSC should be able to meet these managerial requirements with little difficulty. For example, the directors' and shareholders' meetings could be conducted by proxy, and the FSC's principal bank account could be established with a foreign branch of a U.S. bank.

In addition, certain economic processes with respect to each transaction must take place outside the United States.[69] These economic processes requirements are satisfied with respect to any transaction if the FSC, or any related or unrelated person acting under contract with the FSC, participates in the solicitation negotiation, *or* making of the contract outside the United States (sales activities test); and performs activities outside the United States accounting for 50 percent of the direct costs associated with all five specified categories of activities relating to the disposition of export property, or 85 percent of the direct costs associated with each of two of the activities (direct costs test).[70] The five activities are: (1) advertising and sales promotion; (2) processing of customer orders and arranging for delivery; (3) transportation from the time of acquisition by the FSC, or the beginning of a commission relationship, until delivery to the customer; (4) determination and transmittal of a final invoice or statement and the receipt of payment; and (5) assumption of credit risk.[71]

Use of the administrative pricing rules also is keyed into these economic processes requirements. In order to use the administrative pricing rules, an FSC or its agent must perform all the above sales and direct costs activities, although for this purpose the activities may be performed within or without the United States.[72] An FSC, however, is exempted from this requirement for export property which was transferred from a related supplier to a DISC before December 31, 1984 and sold by the FSC after the DISC's termination,[73] and certain binding agreements executed prior to January 1, 1985.[74]

SATISFYING THE ECONOMIC PROCESSES REQUIREMENTS[75]

As a general rule companies engaged in export transactions should be able to meet both the sales activities test and the direct costs test without much difficulty. It will be necessary, however, for an FSC dealing with its related supplier under the administrative pricing rules rather than at arm's length to enter into written agreements which provide that other parties are performing all the export activities on behalf of the FSC and for an arm's length charge. It is not certain whether this charge must include a profit element. In addition, all personnel charged with operating the FSC should have full knowledge of the procedures that must be followed in order to satisfy the economic processes requirements.

Sales Activities Test

With respect to the "sales activities test," the solicitation and negotiation of a contract may be made through any form of communication, including telephone, telegraph, telex, or mail. The "making of a contract" includes the performance of any of the elements necessary to complete a sale, such as making or accepting a sale. In addition, written confirmation to a customer of an oral agreement which confirms variable contract terms or specifies (directly or by cross reference) additional contract terms is considered the making of a contract.[76]

In performing any of these activities, the FSC may act upon standing instructions from its principal. The location of the solicitation, negotiation, or making of a contract is determined by the place where the FSC or its agent initiates the activity.[77] Thus, acceptance of orders through a computer terminal located in the foreign offices of the FSC (or its agent) would be an easy way to satisfy the sales activity portion of the economic processes requirements. Such acceptance of an order by an FSC, however, must be made directly to a customer.

Direct Costs Test

The direct costs test can be met if at least 85 percent of the FSC's total direct costs related to performing any two of the specified five export activities are attributable to activities performed outside the United States. Most companies, therefore, should be able to meet this test without too much difficulty. It will be necessary, however, for each company to evaluate its exporting operations to determine which two of the five activities can have 85 percent of their costs attributable to activities performed outside the United States.

Generally, the advertising and sales promotion test may be met if the FSC or its agent places advertisements for its products in foreign countries or holds trade shows and customer meetings at foreign locations. The processing of orders and arranging for delivery test may be met if the FSC or its agent notifies the related supplier of the orders and makes transportation arrangements through a forwarding agent from its foreign office. The transportation test may be met if the FSC or its agent acquires the export property and assumes the costs of shipping the property after it has left the United States. If the FSC is acting as a commission agent, this test may be met if the commission relationship begins after the property leaves the United States and the FSC assumes the shipping costs.[78]

The final invoice or statement of account and receipt of payment test may be met if the FSC or its agent assembles the final invoices or statements at a foreign office and mails them to customers from that office, and if it assumes the cost of maintaining the bank account into which the customers' payments are deposited. Such deposits may be made to a U.S. branch of a foreign bank if the funds are immediately transferred to the foreign bank. The assumption of credit risk test may be met if the FSC contractually bears such risk and if the FSC's export income is appropriately reduced when a debt becomes uncollectible. The assumption of credit risk test, however, cannot be satisfied in the third year if no bad debts are incurred over a three year period.[79]

The secretary is authorized to promulgate regulations allowing for the grouping of transactions on the basis of product lines or recognized industry or trade usage.[80] These grouping rules should apply for purposes of satisfying the economic processes requirements and, thus, should ease the burden of meeting these requirements.

SMALL BUSINESS PROVISIONS

Small FSC

A corporation qualifying as an FSC can choose to be treated as a "small FSC" if it files an election to be treated as a small FSC and it is not a member of a controlled group of corporations which includes an FSC (unless the other FSC is a small FSC).[81] The major advantage of small FSC treatment is that a small FSC does not have to comply with the foreign management and economic processes requirements in order to be entitled to FSC benefits.[82] A small FSC, however, only is entitled to FSC tax benefits on $5 million of foreign trading gross receipts.[83]

If a small FSC realizes more than $5 million in foreign trading gross receipts during the year, it cannot terminate its small FSC election and elect FSC or DISC status for the year. The FSC can, however, choose which gross receipts qualify for the $5 million limitation in order to obtain high-profit margin sales to maximize its exempt income. For purposes of applying the $5 million limitation, the foreign gross receipts of affiliated small FSCs are aggregated.[84] Thus, multiple small FSCs cannot be used to circumvent the $5 million foreign trading gross receipts limitation.

Interest Charge DISC

A corporation still may elect to be treated as a DISC under modified rules, which impose an annual interest charge on the cumulative tax liability deferred through the DISC.[85] Under these modified rules, deferral of U.S. taxes only is available for DISC income attributable to export gross receipts of $10 million or less. Receipt of qualified export receipts in excess of $10 million results in a deemed distribution of the income attributable to the excess, although such excess receipts will not disqualify the DISC.[86] Similar to the small FSC, the qualified export receipts of affiliated DISCs are aggregated for purposes of this $10 million limitation.[87] Thus, multiple DISCs cannot be used to circumvent the $10 million export receipts limitation.

Although the present DISC rules generally apply to an interest charge DISC, there are several important differences. First, the incremental rules calling for a deemed distribution of DISC income by reference to a "base period" do not apply to an interest charge DISC.[88] Second, the normal deemed distribution of DISC income is reduced to one-seventeenth (5.9 percent) of the DISC's taxable income.[89] In addition, an interest charge DISC must have a taxable year which conforms to the taxable year of its principal shareholder.[90]

The most significant change, however, is that a deductible interest charge is imposed on the DISC's shareholders based upon their deferred tax liability on earnings retained by the DISC. The interest charge is equal to the average investment yield of Treasury bills with one-year maturity dates sold over a one-year period. Interest is charged with respect to deferred taxes on retained DISC income which is not distributed within one year following the close of the DISC's taxable year. Retained DISC income for one year is considered distributed if distributions in the following year or years exceed the DISC's net income for those years.[91] For small exporters, interest charge DISCs are likely to be attractive due to the low interest rate, one-year time lag and low administrative costs involved, since no U.S. or foreign substance is required.

Qualified tax-free trusts and cooperatives should continue to own DISCs. The interest charge rules permit a trust to operate its DISC with the same tax benefits as under the prior DISC rules. All deemed distributions of the DISC (including any distributions attributable to qualified export receipts in excess of $10 million) and all actual distributions would be received tax free by a qualified trust.[92] In addition, there would be no interest charge on income retained by a DISC for the account of an exempt trust which has no taxes deferred.

TRANSITION FROM DISC TO FSC

On December 31, 1984, the 1984 taxable year of all existing DISCs was deemed terminated, and all DISC elections were deemed revoked.[93] Any accumulated DISC income as of December 31, 1984, which was or will be distributed after that date, is permanently exempt from U.S. taxation. Such distributions are treated as previously taxed income which increases a shareholder's basis in its DISC stock.[94] This forgiveness of U.S. taxation on accumulated DISC income, however, only applies to DISCs which were qualified DISCs on December 31, 1984.[95] In determining whether a DISC was qualified on December 31, 1984, the "qualified export assets test" is waived and related suppliers are not required to pay commissions to a DISC with respect to that year.[96] Otherwise, a DISC must meet all the other requirements set out in the DISC provisions.

The normal deemed distribution rules apply to the DISC's December 31, 1984 deemed terminated year, with two significant modifications. First, if the deemed termination resulted in a short taxable year, the export receipts must be annualized for purposes of computing the incremental distribution.[97] Second, the December 31, 1984 deemed distribution may be included in the shareholder's income in ten equal annual installments (unless the shareholder elects a shorter period).[98] The first annual installment is deemed distributed either in the shareholder's second taxable year beginning in 1984, or the shareholder's first taxable year beginning in 1985 if the shareholder only had one taxable year beginning in 1984.[99]

Section 367 of the Code does not apply to a DISC's transfer of its assets to an FSC if the DISC held the assets on August 4, 1983, and the transfer is completed before January 1, 1986.[100] Thus, a DISC will not recognize gain or loss if such assets are transferred to an FSC in a tax-free transaction. For this purpose, a liquidation of the DISC's assets into a parent corporation followed by the parent's transfer of those assets to the FSC is treated as a tax-free reorganization under section 368(a)(1)(D) of the Code.[101]

OFF-SHORE TRADING OPERATIONS

General Principles

Under Code § § 881 and 882[102] an off-shore trading company ("Tradeco") is taxed at a flat 30 percent rate (or lower treaty rate) on passive income from U.S. sources not effectively connected with a U.S. trade or business, and at the U.S. 46 percent rate on its other "U.S. source income" and certain categories of "foreign source income" effectively connected with a U.S. trade or business. Certain categories of tainted "Subpart F income" also may be passed through to Tradeco as a constructive dividend under § 951. All other income of Tradeco could be indefinitely deferred from U.S. taxation until remitted as dividends to its U.S. parent company or other U.S. shareholders.

The objective for Tradeco thus would be to avoid U.S. source trading income, effectively connected foreign source sales income, and Subpart F income.

Avoidance of U.S. Source Income through Passage of Title Abroad

Under Code § 861 U.S. source income includes income derived from the purchase of personal property outside the United States and its sale within the United States. Under Code § 862 foreign source income includes income derived from the purchase of personal property within the United States and its sale outside the United States.

The courts have held that a "sale" takes place when title is passed. Title passes from the seller to the buyer at the place and time at which the parties mutually intend that it should be transferred.[103]

The Internal Revenue Service has vigorously contended that if a sales transaction is arranged for the primary purpose of tax avoidance, the foregoing rule should not be applied—that the sale should be treated as consummated where the "substance of the sale" occurred. The application of the "substance" rule, however, has been repeatedly rejected by the courts. *A.P. Green Export Company*, 284 F.2d 383 (Ct. Cl. 1960), explicitly held:

> Title passes in a sales transaction as a result of the mutual arrangement of the buyer and the seller, whatever the reason or motivation for the consent. It would be an unjustified distortion of this law for us to disregard the parties' stated intention to pass title outside the United States because they were principally motivated by a desire to avoid a tax. (p. 388)

Thus, by carefully arranging for title passage abroad on all of its sales, Tradeco would earn only foreign source income. On U.S. export sales, title could be passed F.A.S. or F.O.B. port of destination. On sales *into* the United States, shipments could be made F.O.B. or F.A.S. foreign port of shipment. Tradeco, thus, would earn no U.S. source trading income taxable at the general 46 percent rate.

Avoidance of Effectively Connected Foreign Source Income

For operating reasons Tradeco may find it advantageous to establish an office in the United States to coordinate the purchase of goods from various U.S. suppliers for export. If Tradeco were incorporated in a country with which the United States has not executed a tax treaty ("nontreaty country"), such a U.S. office of Tradeco would be deemed a taxable "U.S. trade or business." If Tradeco were incorporated in a country with which the United States has executed a tax treaty ("treaty country"), the risk of such a U.S. office being a taxable "U.S. permanent establishment" would be substantially lower;[104] but this risk could not be eliminated entirely without careful monitoring of that office's activities. The following types of foreign source income could be effectively connected to such an office: (i) rents, royalties, and gains on intangible personal property (patents, trademarks, secret processes and formulas, etc.) derived from the active conduct of a licensing business; (ii) dividends, interest, or gain from stock, bonds, or other debt obligations derived from the active conduct of a licensing business; (iii) certain foreign source sales income.[105] In Tradeco's context foreign source sales income would be susceptible to connection with the U.S. office. A key exception applies, however, if: (i) the property sold by Tradeco is its stock in trade; (ii) the property is sold for use, consumption, or disposition outside the United States; and (iii) an office or other fixed place of business of Tradeco outside the United States "participates materially" in such sales.[106]

A foreign office or other fixed place of business is considered to participate materially in a foreign sale if that office: (i) solicits the order which is the basis for the foreign sale; (ii) negotiates the contract of sale; or (iii) performs significant services incident to the sale which were necessary to its consummation.[107]

If, as would be normally contemplated, a foreign office of Tradeco should engage in the above functions, the U.S. office of Tradeco would be effectively shielded from U.S. tax. It would be immaterial whether Tradeco were incorporated in a treaty country (such as Switzerland or the Netherlands Antilles) or a nontreaty country (such as Bermuda, the Cayman Islands, or Hong Kong).

Exemption of Foreign Source Income under Tax Treaty with Switzerland

Switzerland has a uniquely advantageous treaty with the United States. Under Article III, even though a "Swiss enterprise" may have one or more U.S. offices, the United States has agreed to forfeit tax jurisdiction with respect to the "foreign source income" of such an enterprise.[108] Under Code § 894 a treaty provision is paramount to the effectively connected rules. Thus, if Tradeco were incorporated in Switzerland, it could coordinate its purchase and export of U.S. goods through one or more U.S. offices free of any U.S. tax exposure. (See Rev. Ruling 74-63.) In this case Tradeco would be doubly protected: first, under the foreign office "material participation" rule; second, under the U.S.-Swiss Tax Treaty.

It should be emphasized that in order to qualify as a "Swiss enterprise" entitled to treaty protection, Tradeco would have to be more than a corporate shell. A commercial presence would have to be established in Switzerland, such as a manager, telex machine, secretary, bookkeeper, etc.

Avoidance of Subpart F

Tradeco's income normally would be insulated from U.S. tax until actually brought back to its U.S. shareholders via a dividend distribution. Special rules set forth in Subpart F of the Code (§ 951-64), however, now limit the tax benefits of such an off-shore incorporation. Under these rules certain categories of income are "passed through" Tradeco as a constructive dividend to its U.S. parent even though the income is not distributed.

In general, these Subpart F rules reduce the tax benefits from incorporating foreign trading and service installations which deal with a parent company or related affiliates and foreign investment companies outside the ambit of the foreign personal holding company rules. Their effect is comparatively slight on foreign manufacturing operations, foreign corporations marketing goods locally, and foreign corporations dealing primarily with unrelated parties.

Pass-Through to U.S. Shareholders

Under Subpart F the U.S. shareholders of a controlled foreign corporation must take into their gross income the undistributed earnings of the foreign corporation to the extent that these earnings represent:

(i) Passive income from dividends, interest, rents, etc. ("foreign personal holding company income," with modifications).

(ii) Sales or trading income (including commissions) from purchases and sales of personal property, provided (a) the transaction in-involves a related corporation or controlling stockholder; (b) the goods are manufactured, produced, or grown outside the country in which the foreign corporation is incorporated; and (c) are purchased or sold for use and consumption outside of that country ("foreign base company sales income").

(iii) Income from services performed for related corporations and stockholders outside the country of incorporation of the foreign corporation ("foreign base company services income").

(iv) Income from certain foreign shipping activities ("foreign base company shipping income").

(v) Income from certain oil-related activities ("foreign base company oil-related income").

(vi) Earnings (from any source) invested in certain types of U.S. property.

(vii) Additional Subpart F income arising from participation in an an international boycott or the payment of illegal bribes. [Code § R 952(a)(3) and (4).]

The first five types of income—foreign personal holding company income, foreign base company sales income, foreign base company services income, foreign base company shipping income, and foreign base company oil-related income—comprise "foreign base company income" and must total 10 percent of gross income of the controlled foreign corporation for any part of it to be taxed to the U.S. shareholders. If such income comprises over 70 percent of the gross income of the controlled foreign corporation, all of the earnings of such a base company are passed through to the U.S. shareholders.

Tradeco's primary Subpart F exposure would relate to category (ii) above. Tradeco normally would earn income on sales of goods originating outside its country of incorporation and sold to customers outside that country. Purchases from a parent or affiliate would generate foreign base company sales income. Tradeco, however, would avoid the reach of Subpart F if most of its trading transactions involve goods purchased from unrelated suppliers and sold to unrelated customers. In this connection, a supplier or customer would be "unrelated" unless there were a *greater than* 50 percent voting common stock nexus between Tradeco and such a party (either as a parent company, subsidiary, or sister company). A joint-venture company in which Tradeco or its parent company held a 50 percent or lower voting stock interest would be deemed an unrelated supplier.

Investment by Tradeco in U.S. Property

Under § 956 of the Code, Tradeco's U.S. shareholders would be taxed directly to the extent that Tradeco's earnings were invested in "U.S. property." This is the sixth category of "Subpart F income" income outlined above.

Excerpted from the definition of "U.S. property" are:

1. U.S. bonds, money, or bank accounts;
2. property bought in the United States for export to or use in foreign countries;
3. an obligation of a U.S. person arising in connection with the sale or processing of property if the amount does not exceed that which is ordinary and necessary to carry on the business of both parties to the transaction;
4. any aircraft, railroad rolling stock, vessel, motor vehicle, or container used in the transportation of persons or property in foreign commerce and used predominantly outside the United States;
5. stock or debt obligations of a U.S. domestic corporation, provided such a domestic corporation is not a 10 percent or greater shareholder of Tradeco, or a corporation in which Tradeco's shareholders hold, directly or indirectly, a 25 percent or greater voting stock interest.

The above categories of exceptions would leave Tradeco broad latitude. For example, under (1) Tradeco could deposit its excess cash in a U.S. bank account and draw interest tax free; under (2) it could acquire U.S. inventory; under (3) it could make arm's length advances to a U.S. supplier. Finally, under (5) Tradeco could use its accumulated earnings to make stock investment in and loans to unrelated U.S. companies. If Tradeco were incorporated in a treaty country it could earn such investment income from U.S. sources subject to reduced U.S. withholding rates.

Potential Tradeco Exposure under General U.S. Tax Rules

"Sham" Doctrine

In a number of cases, the U.S. Internal Revenue Service has taken the position that a corporate entity that does not perform bona fide business activities is a "sham" and is to be disregarded as a viable legal entity for federal income tax purposes. If this argument is used successfully by the Internal Revenue Service to "pierce the corporate veil," the income earned by the corporation is attributed to its stockholders for U.S. income tax purposes.

At the same time, it is axiomatic that a taxpayer has the right to arrange its business affairs in any manner it chooses. This basic concept is inherent in the tax law. A taxpayer may operate its business as an unincorporated proprietorship, a partnership, one or more corporations, or any other form of business organization. When the taxpayer selects a corporation as the proper form of business organization, that corporation cannot be disregarded as a separate legal entity for tax purposes if the corporation *actually performs business activities*. This cardinal principle was made clear in the leading case of *Moline Properties, Inc. v. Commissioner*, wherein the Supreme Court stated [(319) U.S. 436, 438 (1943)] :

> The doctrine of corporate entity fills a useful purpose in business life. Whether the purpose be to gain an advantage under the law of the state of incorporation or to avoid or to comply with the demands of creditors or to serve the creator's personal or undisclosed convenience, so long as that purpose is the equivalent of business activity or is followed by the carrying on of business by the corporation, the corporation remains a separate taxable entity.

Clearly this principle enunciated by the Supreme Court has as much validity in its application to foreign business activities as it does to domestic business activities, as indicated by the following statement by the U.S. Tax Court:

> The question . . . is not to be clouded by the use of a foreign corporation rather than a domestic corporation, to escape United States Taxation, except as it may bear on the question whether that corporation was in fact "formed for a substantial business purpose or actually engaged in substantial business activity."[109]

Similarly, in *Nat Harrison Associates, Inc.,* 42 T.C. 601 (1964), *acq.*, 1965-2 C.B. 5, which involved the validity as a separate legal entity of a Panamanian corporation organized by the partners of a domestic partnership to conduct all business activities outside the United States, the Tax Court stated, citing the *Moline Properties* case:

> This was a natural division of the business . . . Whether the primary reason for its existence and conduct of business was to avoid U.S. taxes or to permit more economical performance of contracts through use of native labor, or a combination of these and other reasons, makes no difference in this regard. Any one of these reasons would constitute a valid business purpose for its existence and conduct of business as long as it actually conducted business.

It seems clear under the *Moline Properties* case and other cases above that if Tradeco *actually engages in business activities* the Internal Revenue Service must recognize it as a separate legal entity for tax purposes. Provided Tradeco has an office outside the United States and engages in actual purchase and resale activities, there should be no question that it be treated as a viable legal entity for U.S. income tax purposes.

"Assignment of Income" Doctrine

It is a well-established principle of tax law enunciated in *Lucas v. Earl*, 281 111 (1931), and subsequent decisions that income is to the person who earns the income and that such a person cannot make an anticipatory assignment of the income to avoid the tax thereon. This principle is commonly referred to as the "asisignment of income" doctrine.

The assignment of income argument was made by the Internal Revenue Service in the *Nat Harrison* case in seeking to attribute to the domestic partnership the income earned by the Panamanian corporation from the performance of certain construction contracts entered into by the partnership. The partnership obtained the performance bond and paid the premiums due thereon, purchased material for the jobs, and supplied administrative facilities and administrative and engineering services. The partnership also remained liable as the prime contractor under the contracts. Nevertheless, the Tax Court rejected the Internal Revenue Service's argument, stating:

> Respondent also argues that Associates [the partnership], as the prime contractor, had control of the flow of income and complete discretion over the disposition thereof [citing *Lucas v. Earl* and other similar cases] . . . In each of those cases the Court found that the assignor of the income had either actually performed the work and earned the income or owned the property which produced the income . . . While Associates remained the prime contractor here, *the contracts themselves did not produce the income. It was the work performed that do so . . . And we have held that a taxpayer's right to designate the party to earn income does not constitute such control over the income that it should be imputed to him, and that the designation does not constitute the anticipatory assignment of income . . .*

Obviously, the key under the *Nat Harrison* case to avoiding the application of the assignment of income doctrine to attribute Tradeco's income to its U.S. parent company is the *actual performance* by Tradeco of the purchase and resale activities giving rise to the income through its own foreign office employees.

Section 482

Section 482 of the Code allows the Internal Revenue Service to allocate income or deductions involving transactions between related entities if it determines that such an allocation is necessary in order to prevent evasion of taxes or to clearly reflect the income of the entities involved in the transactions.

The Internal Revenue Service's authority under § 482 is quite broad and in general terms covers any situation where the parties have not dealt at "arm's length," including intercompany loans, performance of services, and the transfer of use of tangible or intangible property.

If Tradeco's activities are conducted entirely with unrelated parties (i.e., purchases from and sales to unrelated persons), no problems should arise under § 482. However, to the extent that Tradeco has dealings with any related persons, care should be taken to assure that such dealings are at arm's length. In this connection Tradeco should maintain good contemporaneous documentation in support of the arm's length nature of any transactions with its parent or affiliates.

Constructive Dividends

The Internal Revenue Service has frequently taken the position that transactions involving the expenditure of funds or other action by a corporation for the direct or indirect benefit of a stockholder entail constructive dividends. Thus, for example, the Internal Revenue Service takes the position that a bargain sale of assets by a corporation (Tradeco) to a stockholder (its parent) produces a constructive dividend to the stockholder equal to the bargain element. Similarly, the expenditure of funds by a corporation for the benefit of a stockholder gives rise to a constructive dividend to the stockholder.

Obviously, constructive dividends can be avoided by minimizing transactions and expenditures between Tradeco and its parent or affiliates.

Tax Benefits Achieved through Tradeco

Tradeco could earn and accumulate income at tax rates in the 6 to 15 percent range. (See the discussion of foreign tax regimes below.) Tradeco's business could thus grow on 90-cent dollars, rather than 54-cent dollars (after 46 percent tax) normally available to a U.S. company. Assuming $1,000,000 in export sales, a 10 percent profit margin, and an effective 10 percent tax rate, Tradeco would net $90,000 after tax annually. As illustrated below, to achieve the same after-tax return a U.S. company selling through a subsidiary Foreign Sales Corporation ("FSC") would have to generate an additional 48 percent in export sales ($1,480,000); while a conventional domestic corporation would have to generate an additional 67 percent in export sales ($1,670,000). (See Table 6.1.)

Table 6.1

	Off-Shore Corp.	FSC	U.S. Corp.
Sales	1,000,000	1,410,660	1,666,670
Operating income (10 percent)	100,000	147,783	166,667
Tax	10,000 (10 percent)	57,783	76,667 (46 percent)
		(39.1 percent)*	
After-tax profit	90,000	90,000	90,000

*Under the FSC regime 85 percent of the FSC's trading income is subject to a U.S. 46 percent tax, yielding an overall rate of 39.1 percent.

Off-Shore Tax

Summarized below are tax benefits achievable in leading off-shore trading jurisdictions:

Netherlands Antilles

In the Netherlands Antilles trading company rulings can be negotiated in Curacao to assure a tax of not more than 6 percent on net operating profits and in Aruba to assure a tax of not more than 3 percent on such profits.

Cayman Islands

In the Cayman Islands a trading company would pay no tax.

Bermuda

In Bermuda a trading company would pay no tax.

Hong Kong

In Hong Kong a trading company would be taxed at the rate of 18.5 percent on its net income.

Switzerland

Switzerland provides the best combination of favorable tax rates, acceptable customs position, market proximity, and general quality of business climate in Western Europe. Switzerland is the only major country in Western Europe which would permit order acceptance and conclusion of contracts by a local office without triggering full domestic tax rates. On the other hand, Switzerland maintains tight controls on the inflow of foreign employees, and work permit quotas are strictly enforced by each canton.

Switzerland levies federal, cantonal, and municipal taxes. The cantonal and municipal taxes, which vary from place to place, are the major corporate taxes. The federal tax burden of 9.8 percent is uniform and relatively light. Tax incidence can be modified substantially by the selection of one canton over another. In each case the company's tax status is negotiated in advance with cantonal officials. Examples of the kind of treatment which may be available are as follows:

Zug: Zug is conveniently located near the Zurich airport. Many foreign companies have located subsidiaries or branches there. In Zug the cantonal rate of 17 percent would apply to all Swiss source income. However, only one-quarter of the cantonal tax is levied on foreign source income, provided it constitutes 80 percent or more of the branch's total income. If all the branch's income were from foreign sources the combined federal/cantonal rate would be 14.05 percent (9.8 percent Federal Defense Tax plus 4.25 percent cantonal tax).

Basel: Basel, 45 miles northwest of Zurich on the German border, applies rules similar to those of Zug. Swiss source income is taxed at the ordinary 27 percent cantonal rate. For cantonal tax purposes, the authorities usually agree that only one-tenth of the cantonal tax is to be levied, giving an effective cantonal tax rate of 2.7 percent. Together with the federal tax rate of 9.8 percent, the aggregate income tax burden on income would be approximately 12.5 percent.

Fribourg: Fribourg, approximately 75 miles midway between Zurich and Geneva, would appear to be the most generous in granting tax privileges, provided that most of the company's income is generated from foreign sources. Under these circumstances, the cantonal tax authorities fully exempt foreign source income from cantonal tax, leaving only the Federal Defense Tax burden of 9.8 percent.

Geneva: Geneva, on the French border, grants tax privileges to companies or branches deriving most of their income from sources outside Switzerland. The cantonal tax rate is a flat 9 percent, yielding a combined federal and cantonal rate of 18.8 percent.

Vaud (Lausanne): The tax authorities of the canton Vaud, contiguous to Geneva, usually agree that only one-fifth of the 30 percent cantonal rate is to be levied, yielding an effective rate of 6 percent. This rate, combined with the federal rate of 9.8 percent, results in a total burden of 15.8 percent.

THE EXPORT TRADING COMPANY ACT OF 1982

President Reagan signed the Export Trading Company Act (the "Act") on October 8, 1982.[110] It has been heralded as the legislation that will reverse our trade deficit imbalances, create thousands of jobs in the United States,[111] and rejuvenate the entrepreneurial spirit that is essential for creative and successful export trade ventures. It is unlikely that it will single-handedly accomplish these achievements, but it is clear that the Act can have a pervasive and long-term effect on export trade activities in the United States.

The overall purpose of the Act is to increase the export of products and services offered by U.S. companies, thus decreasing trade deficits and increasing the general economic health of the country. It attempts to accomplish this purpose by fulfilling the following objectives: changing existing laws, such as antitrust laws,[112] that deter export trade activities; allowing certain banking-affiliated institutions to invest in export trade companies; increasing trade financing by financial institutions; increasing the access to and the efficient use of management, marketing, and financing expertise and resources required for export trade activities; and increasing government services and resources aimed at developing export trade activities.

The Act is divided into four major parts:

Title I introduces the Act's general purposes and establishes a government office for fostering the achievement of these purposes.

Title II specifies the standards by which bank-affiliated institutions may invest in export trading companies, authorizes Export-Import Bank loan guarantees, and liberalizes the use of bankers' acceptances in trade activities.

Title III delineates the procedures by which an export trade activity may receive immunity from the antitrust laws by receiving a "certificate of review" from the Secretary of Commerce.

Title IV summarizes the standards for determining whether export trade activities violate the antitrust laws.

Introduction to the Act and Export Trading Companies

Title I introduces the Act by summarizing facts on which the legislation is premised. Specifically, it describes problems that have hindered the growth of export trade activities, and explains the relationship between increasing export trade activities and creating jobs. It also authorizes the establishment of an office within the Department of Commerce to provide information and contacts for those interested in export trade and export trading companies.

The Act is filled with "terms of art" so that the common definition of a term may be inappropriate. Title I defines some of the key terms of the Act.[113] For example, "export trading company" is defined in § 103(4) as a profit or nonprofit organization which is established and operating "principally" for the purposes of exporting goods or services produced in the United States, or facilitating the export of goods or services of unaffiliated persons by providing export trade services.

The export trade company ("ETC") is a major vehicle for accomplishing the goals of the Act. It is an organization which would serve as direct exporters of goods and services produced in the United States;[114] or would act as an intermediary between unaffiliated U.S. producers and foreign markets and would offer expert "export trade services" to less experienced U.S. producers.[115]

The Act anticipates that the growth of ETCs will come primarily from the formation of new ETCs by banking-affiliated organizations and major corporations, and secondarily from the accelerated development of existing trading companies and similar entities.[116] ETCs may take a variety of forms.[117] Examples include national or regional associations of producers of the same product or service, formed to share marketing or production costs and management expertise. Also, an ETC may be organized by all participants in a specific large-scale export project, each contributing its unique service or product to the enterprise. Another ETC may be owned by a group of regional bank holding companies or be formed by bank holding companies and nonbank partners. Other export trading companies may be characterized as:

1. *product specific*—with either a national or regional base; this variation would specialize into particular products or product groups;
2. *geographic-specific*—these would serve a specific foreign area from a national or regional base;
3. *consortium*—with either banking or nonbanking equity participation, these would concentrate on turnkey projects;
4. *piggyback*—these would build around the existing distribution and marketing systems of a U.S.-based multinational company.

Participation of Banking-Affiliated Institutions in Export Trading Companies

The purpose of Title II is "to provide for meaningful and effective participation by bank holding companies, bankers' banks, and Edge Act corporations in the financing and development of export trading companies in the United States."[118] It may be cited as the "Bank Export Services Act" and amends provisions of the Bank Holding Company Act of 1956. This means that other investment restrictions imposed by the Bank Holding Company Act on bank-affiliated institutions would automatically apply to investments in ETCs.

In addition, the Act provides other policy and procedural guidelines for the Board of Governors of the Federal Reserve System to use in promoting the bank's financial "safety and soundness." For example, the Board of Governors may forbid a proposed investment only if it would be an "unsafe or unsound" banking practice, or it would have "materially adverse effect on the safety and soundness" of a subsidiary bank, or inadequate information on the proposed investment is provided.

A summary of other guidelines follows: (1) A subsidiary of a bank holding company which is an Edge Act Corporation or agreement corporation may invest up to 5 percent of its consolidated capital and surplus in one or more ETC. (2) A bank holding company cannot extend more than 10 percent of its capital and surplus as credit to an ETC. (3) The bank-affiliated institution cannot offer more favorable consideration or terms to an ETC than it would to another entity, in a similar situation.

In addition, the Act increases the ceiling amount of bankers' acceptances that may be used. Although liberalizing the use of bankers' acceptances, the Act acknowledges that subsequent regulatory guidelines may be appropriate.[119]

An ETC in which a bank has invested can offer essentially the same "export trade services" as any other ETC and thus serve as an intermediary between U.S. producers and foreign markets. However, it cannot be the producer of the products or services, except for performing some "incidental product modification." It also is subject to restrictions on its securities investment activities.

Export-Import Bank Loan Guarantees

Finally, Title II authorizes the Export-Import Bank to provide guarantees for loans given by financial creditors to ETCs or to other exporters. These guarantees are available if they are deemed to facilitate export activities and if the private credit market proves to be inadequate. Furthermore, a major portion of the guarantees should go to small, medium-size, and minority businesses or agricultural concerns.

Immunity from Antitrust Laws through a Certification Process

Title III of the Act authorizes the Secretary of Commerce to issue a "certificate of review," which would give certain immunity from antitrust laws to the specified export trade activities of an ETC or any other applicant. Unless the activities pose "clear and irreparable harm to the national interest," the export trade activities would be completely immune from federal government prosecution.[120] If the federal government determines, however, that the substantive standards required for certification are no longer complied with, it may revoke the certification following a specified procedural process.

The Act does provide a private cause of action for any U.S. person who has been injured by the certificate holder's failure to comply with the substantive standards required for certification.[121] The damages, however, are limited to actual damages (not treble), loss of interest on damages, and the costs of the suit. Also note that two provisions in the Act will discourage frivolous suits against certificate holders: (1) a certificate holder enjoys the presumption that its conduct does not violate the substantive standards, so the potential plaintiff would have a difficult burden of proof; and (2) if the plaintiff is not successful, the defendant certificate holder will be awarded its costs including attorney's fees.

Substantive and Procedural Standards for Certification Process

The Secretary of Commerce will issue the certificate of review if the applicant complies with specified procedural standards and substantive standards. Section 303(a) lists the substantive standards. It requires that the export trade activities will:

1. result in neither a substantial lessening of competition or restraint of trade within the United States nor a substantial restraint of the export trade of any competitor of the applicant;
2. not unreasonably enhance, stabilize, or depress prices within the United States of the goods, wares, merchandise, or services of the class exported by the applicant;
3. not constitute unfair methods of competition against competitors engaged in the export of goods, wares, merchandize, or services of the class exported by the applicant; and
4. not include any act that may reasonably be expected to result in the sale for consumption or resale within the United States of the goods, wares, merchandise, or services exported by the applicant.

Sections 302 and 303 describe the procedural requirements. A successful compliance with the requirements is summarized as follows: Written application to the Secretary of Commerce is received. Announcement of application is published in the Federal Register (within 10 days of receipt of publication). Determination by the Secretary of Commerce, in consultation with the Attorney General, of whether substantive standards of Section 303(a) are met, is made (within 90 days). Issuance of a certificate of review is accomplished with any terms and conditions necessary for compliance with substantive standards. Expedited process is possible (although the minimum time requirement is at least 30 days after the announcement of application in the Federal Register).

Provisions for the notification of denial of the application and appeal procedures are also given.

Exemptions for Export Trade Activities under Amendments to the Antitrust Laws

Title IV of the Act, cited as the "Foreign Trade Antitrust Improvements Act of 1982," amends the Sherman Act and the Federal Trade Commission Act. It offers an alternative to those who choose not to apply for a certificate of review.

In summary, Title IV states that trade activities will not be subject to antitrust prosecution unless the activities have a "direct, substantial, and reasonably foreseeable effect" on commerce in the United States, on import commerce to the United States, or on the export activities of a person "engaged in such trade or commerce in the United States." It therefore appears to exempt all trade activities of ETCs or non-ETC entities which have no effect on domestic commerce or domestic competition. Although the meaning of these terms is unclear,[122] some have predicted that these Title IV provisions will be the key to protection against antitrust prosecution for export activities.[123]

Conclusion and Implications for Multinational Companies

The Export Trading Company Act signals policy changes in the government's attitude toward export trade activities and banking functions. Its purpose is to vigorously promote export trade activities through the use of several related approaches: (1) forming export trading companies, (2) allowing bank-affiliated institutions to invest in and extend credit to export trading companies and export ventures, (3) offering a certification process by which export trade activities will have some immunity from the antitrust laws, and (4) changing the antitrust laws to exempt export activities which have no effect on domestic competition.

The Act recognizes that successful export ventures require large infusions of capital, access to external financing, international financial expertise, sophisticated communications, and contacts with both foreign markets and U.S. producers of goods and services. The participation of banking institutions and the formation of ETCs can contribute substantially to providing these essential ingredients. The Act attempts to remove two major obstacles to forming export trading companies: prohibition against bank investment and uncertainty about the application of U.S. antitrust laws.

Several large multinational companies formed export trading entities even before the enactment of the Act. How the Act will affect those companies remains to be seen. Other multinational companies, however, may clearly benefit from the formation of ETCs. For instance, U.S. corporations already exporting to certain foreign countries could form an export trading company and pool their resources and expertise. Furthermore, having familiarity with market conditions in those countries, they could handle goods and services of other U.S. firms, thus resulting in lower overhead costs and economics of scale in distribution for all participants.

As another example, large U.S. electrical equipment manufactures and major U.S. engineering firms could form an export trading company to bid jointly on a hydroelectric project in a foreign country. Finally, counter trade and other forms of barter trade are growing dramatically as forms of international trade. Large U.S. multinationals will require assistance in the financing and resale of goods that have been received through barter, and ETCs affiliated with large banking institutions could help facilitate these activities.

NOTES

1. Income allocated by the exporter to the DISC reduces the exporter's taxable income and, thus, is effectively deductible.

2. Property containing foreign-manufactured components is deemed to be "export property" if no more than 50 percent of its export value is attributable to components imported into the United States.

3. If individual shareholders own the DISC, the deemed distribution is reduced to 50 percent.

4. Export profit	$100
Allocated to DISC	$ 50
Deemed distributed by DISC (57.5 percent)	$ 28.75
Retained by DISC and tax deferred	$ 21.25
U.S. tax on export profit (46 percent X 78.75) effective rate on export profit)	$ 36.225 (36.2 percent

5. For a DISC's taxable years beginning before 1980, the base period was 1972-75. For 1980 and succeeding years the base period rolls forward one year, i.e., 1973-76 for 1980, 1974-77 for 1981, and so forth.

6. *Senate Comm. on Finance, 98th Cong., 2d Sess., Explanation of Deficit Reduction Act of 1984* 634-35 (Comm. Print 1984) [hereinafter cited as *Senate Report*].

7. Rules for a commission basis FSC are to be prescribed in regulations. 1954 Int. Rev. Code, § § 924(d)(4), 925(b)(1). Unless otherwise noted, all section references hereafter are to the 1954 Int. Rev. Code.

8. A DISC itself is not subject to tax, but 57.5 percent and 50 percent of its income generally was taxed currently to its corporate and noncorporate shareholders, respectively, as a deemed distribution.

9. Treas. Reg. § § 1.993-1(a), 1.993-1(1)(1).

10. § § 922(a), 441(h).

11. For FSC purposes, a possession of the United States does not include Puerto Rico. § 927(d)(5).

12. Several companies may pool together and establish a shared FSC. For example, a business association could establish an FSC for its members.

13. An office must constitute a "permanent establishment" under income tax treaty concepts. More than one FSC may share an office, however, and an FSC's office need not be located in the country in which the FSC is incorporated. *Senate Report* at 637.

14. If any controlled group of corporations which includes a DISC established an FSC, then the DISC is treated as having terminated its DISC status. Temp. Treas. Reg. § 1.921-1T(b)(13); § 805(b)(5) of the 1984 Tax Act.

15. If an FSC's principal shareholder changes its annual accounting period, or if its voting power is reduced by at least 10 percent and it no longer is the FSC's principal shareholder, the FSC must change its annual accounting period accordingly. The voting power of the principal shareholder is determined as of the beginning of the FSC's taxable year. Temp. Treas. Reg. § 1.921-1T(b)(6).

16. At least 95 percent of a DISC's income must constitute qualified export receipts, and at least 95 percent of its assets at the close of its taxable year must constitute qualified export assets. § § 992(a)(1)(A), (a)(1)(B).

17. § 927(f)(1)(A).

18. Temp. Treas. Reg. § 1.921-1T(b)(1).

19. Temp. Treas. Reg. § 1.921-1T(b)(4).

20. § 923(b).

21. Compare § 924(a) and § 993(a).

22. § 924(a).

23. § § 924(f), 923(a)(5).

24. Compare § 927(a)(1) and § 993(c)(1).

25. The destination test is satisfied if the FSC delivers the property to a carrier or freight forwarder for ultimate delivery, use, or consumption outside of the United States without regard to the F.O.B. point or place or passage of title, whether the purchaser is a U.S. or foreign purchaser, or whether the property is for use of the purchaser or for resale. *Senate Report* at 652. See also Treas. Reg. § 1.993-3(d)(2).

26. The fair market value of any article imported into the United States is its appraised value upon importation, as determined under § 402 of the Tariff Act of 1930 (19 U.S.C. § 1401a). *Senate Report* at 652. See also Treas. Reg. § 1.993-3(e)(4)(i), but note that the FSC regulations are not required to follow the DISC regulations for determining the foreign content of any product. *Senate Report* at 652-53.

27. Compare § 927(a)(2), (a)(3), and § 993(c)(2), (c)(3).

28. Compare § 994(a)(1) and § 925(a). In order to use the administrative pricing rules, however, an FSC or its agent must engage (within or without the United States) in all the sales and direct costs activities of the economic processes requirements. See infra notes 64-69 and accompanying text.

29. §§ 925(a), (d). Limiting the 1.83 percent method to twice the amount allowable under the 23 percent method effectively incorporates the DISC "no-loss" rule. See Treas. Reg. § 1.994-1(e)(1). The secretary also is directed to promulgate marginal costing rules for determining combined taxable income under the 23 percent method. § 925(b)(2). These rules should operate in much the same manner at the DISC marginal costing rules. See Treas. Reg. § 1.994-2.

30. Gross export sales $100.00
    Operating profit margin (8 percent) $ 8.00
    23 percent X export profit ($8) $ 1.84
    1.83 percent X sale price ($100) $ 1.83

If the operating profit margin is less than 8 percent, 1.83 percent of gross sales will exceed 23 percent of export profits.

31. § 927(d)(2)(B).

32. See Treas. Reg. § 1.994-1(c)(7).

33. §§ 923(a)(3), 291(a)(4)(B). Any deductions of the FSC are allocated on a proportionate basis between the FSC's exempt and nonexempt foreign trade income. § 921(b). Since exempt foreign trade income is an exclusion from an FSC's gross income, deductions allocable to exempt foreign trade income may not be used to reduce an FSC's taxable income.

34. §§ 923(a)(2), 291(a)(4)(A).

35. § 921(a).

36. §§ 881, 882.

37. § 951(e). The secretary also is authorized to exclude property related to the export activities to an FSC from the subpart F rules relating to investments in U.S. property. Ibid. § 956(b)(2)(I). Generally, under the subpart F rules the U.S. shareholders of a controlled foreign corporation are taxed constructively on the foreign corporation's trading income earned on purchases from a parent or affiliate for resale abroad and on investment income, and investments in U.S. property. Ibid. § 951(a)(1).

38. § 245(c)(1).

39. §§ 296(b), 882(a)(1), 871(b).

40. § 921(d)(1).

41. § 882(a)(1).

42. § 951(e).

43. § 245(c)(1). An FSC's foreign trade income must be carefully computed under the safe harbor rules, since any income allocated to an FSC in excess of the amount permitted may be subject to double taxation; first, in the hands of the FSC and, second, upon distribution to the FSC's shareholders. Pending issuance of regulations, however, such distribution may be treated as out of non-exempt income and, therefore, subject to the 100 percent dividends received deduction.

44. § 926(b).

45. §§ 921(a), 951(e), 245(c)(1), 926(b).

46. §§ 921(d), 951(e).

47. §§ 921(d)(2), (d)(3), 882(a)(1).

48. § 245(c)(2).

49. For subpart F purposes, an FSC's investment income and carrying charges are treated as U.S. source income. § 951(e)(1). Subpart F income does not include any item of income from U.S. sources which is effectively connected with a U.S. trade or business. § 952(b).

50. §§ 921(d), 951(e).

51. §§ 901(h), 906(b)(5).

52. § 904(d)(1)(C).

53. §§ 901(h), 906(b)(5); *Senate Report* at 639.

54. § 904(d)(1)(D).

55. A taxpayer's allowable foreign tax credit is limited by the following formula:

$$\frac{\text{Foreign source taxable income}}{\text{worldwide taxable income}} \quad X \quad \begin{array}{c}\text{U.S. tax} \\ \text{on worldwide} \\ \text{taxable income}\end{array}$$

§ 904(a). Thus, any increase in foreign source income increases the limitation.

56. § 927(e)(1). When a U.S. exporter passes title outside the United States on its export sales, generally 50 percent of its taxable income from the sales is foreign source income. § 863(b)(2). Without the FSC special rule governing source of income, a U.S. exporter selling export property through an FSC at a profit of $100 would have total income of $77 if it uses the 23 percent FSC pricing rule and foreign source income of $38.50. This rule limits the U.S. exporter's foreign source income to $25, one-half of the total income which could have been earned by the U.S. exporter under the DISC 50-50 income allocation rule ($50).

57. *Senate Report* at 655.

58. § 922(a)(1)(A). Note that a bill was introduced in the last Congress which would have made it mandatory for FSCs to locate in a U.S. possession. H.R. 6104, 98th Cong., 2d Sess. (1984).

59. § 927(d)(5).

60. § 927(e)(3). The list released by the Treasury on November 6, 1984, certified the following countries:

Australia	Germany	New Zealand
Austria	Iceland	Norway
Belgium	Ireland	Pakistan

Canada	Jamaica	Philippines
Denmark	Korea	South Africa
Egypt	Malta	Sweden
Finland	Morocco	Trinidad and Tobago
France	Netherlands	

61. An FSC may not claim the benefits of any income tax treaty between the United States and any other foreign country. § 927(e)(4).

62. Assume an FSC is incorporated in a foreign country where its income is subject to an effective 10 percent foreign tax rate. If the FSC and its related supplier earn $1 million in total pretax export profits, under the administrative pricing rules 15 percent or $150,000 would be exempt from U.S. taxation, resulting in a U.S. tax savings of $69,000. Noncreditable foreign taxes imposed on the FSC would be $23,000 ($230,000 allocated to the FSC times 10 percent). Thus, the total U.S. tax savings would be reduced to $46,000 ($69,000 minus $23,000).

63. § 927(e)(5). The U.S. Virgin Islands, Guam, and the Northern Mariana Islands have passed legislation which extend favorable tax treatment to FSCs beyond December 31, 1986. American Samoa has proposed similar legislation.

64. Jamaica has announced that such legislation passed. Belgium and the Netherlands have announced that taxes will be imposed only upon a small increment of an FSC's income equal to a percentage (5 to 8 percent) of its operating expenses.

65. See discussion below.

66. Temp. Treas. Reg. § § 1.921-1T(b)(8)-(b)(10), (b)(12). See also § 805 (a) (2) of the 1984 Tax Act.

67. § 924(b)(1)(A).

68. § 924(c).

69. § 924(b)(1)(B).

70. § 924(c).

71. § 924(e).

72. § 925(c). See *Senate Report* at 646.

73. Temp. Treas. Reg. § 1.921-1T(b)(11).

74. § 805(a)(2) of the 1984 Tax Act; Temp. Treas. Reg. § 1.921-1T(b) (8)-(b)(10).

75. The discussion on this subject is based upon the *Senate Report*.

76. *Senate Report* at 641.

77. Ibid.

78. Ibid. at 642-43.

79. Ibid. at 644-45.

80. § 927(d)(2)(B).

81. § 922(b). The timing requirements for making a small FSC election are the same as those for a regular FSC election. § 927(f)(1)(A); Temp. Treas. Reg. § 1.921-1T(b)(1).

82. § 924(b)(2)(A). In order to use the administrative pricing rules, however, a small FSC or its agent must engage (within or without the United States) in all the sales and direct costs activities of the economic processes requirements.

83. § 924(b)(2)(B)(i). If a small FSC has a short taxable year in 1985 because it elects to be treated as a small FSC prior to the beginning of its principal shareholder's taxable year, the $5 million limitation on foreign trading gross receipts is to be prorated on a daily basis. Temp. Treas. Reg. § 1.921-1T(b)(5).

84. § 924(b)(2)(B).

85. The timing requirements for making an interest charge DISC election are the same as those for an FSC or small FSC. § 992(b)(1); Temp. Treas. Reg. § 1.921-1T(b)(1).

86. § 995(b)(1)(E).

87. § 995(b)(4).

88. Compare ibid. § 955(b)(1)(E) before and after its amendment by the Tax Act.

89. § 995(b)(1)(F)(i). Prior to their amendment by the Tax Act, §§ 995 (b)(1)(F)(i) and 291(a)(4) of the Code provided for a normal deemed distribution of 57.5 percent for corporate shareholders and 50 percent for noncorporate shareholders.

90. § 441(h). The same rules applicable to a change in the accounting period or voting power of an FSC's principal shareholder apply to an interest charge DISC's principal shareholder. Temp. Treas. Reg. § 1.921-T(b)(6).

91. § 995(f).

92. § 501(a).

93. § 805(b)(1)(A) of the 1984 Tax Act; Temp. Treas. Reg. § 1.921-1T (a)(1).

94. § 805(b)(2)(A) of the 1984 Tax Act; § 996(e)(1); Temp. Treas. Reg. § 1.921-1(a)(7). A deficiency or qualifying distribution which is made to satisfy the qualified export receipts test for a DISC's December 31, 1984 taxable year, however, is not treated as previously taxed income. Temp. Treas. Reg. §§ 1.921-1T(a)(8), (a)(9).

95. § 805(b)(2)(B) of the 1984 Tax Act. If a DISC was disqualified, but had requalified as of December 31, 1984, any accumulated DISC income previously required to be taken into income upon the prior disqualification is not entitled to forgiveness from U.S. taxation. All accumulated DISC income earned subsequent to reclassification, however, is entitled to forgiveness. Temp. Treas. Reg. § 1.921-1T(a)(6).

96. § 805(b)(1)(A) of the 1984 Tax Act; Temp. Treas. Reg. § 1.921-1T (a)(3), (a)(4).

97. Temp. Treas. Reg. § 1.921-1T(a)(2).

98. § 805(b)(3) of the 1984 Tax Act; Temp. Treas. Reg. § 1.921-1T(a) (10). Although the transition rules of the Tax Act only permit the ten-year installment treatment where the DISC and its shareholders had different fiscal years, the temporary regulations do not appear to be so limited.

99. Temp. Treas. Reg. § 1.921-1T(a)(10). A DISC shareholder is required to attach a statement to its tax return for its first taxable for which an installment is deemed distributed, indicating the period over which it will spread its pro rata share of the December 31, 1984 deemed distribution. Ibid.

100. Ibid. § 1.921-1T(b)(7).

101. Ibid.

102. All code references are to the U.S. 1954 Internal Revenue Code.

103. Where the parties fail to express their intent, the law of sales prescribes various presumptions of intent, generally to the effect that title or ownership passes F.O.B. factory or at the original point of shipment where the seller is not required by contract to make actual delivery at destination. It is, of course, essential that such a presumption be rebutted by express agreement to the contrary between Tradeco and its customer.

104. Under many U.S. tax treaties, a U.S. taxable permanent establishment specifically excludes a U.S. office established for the purpose of purchasing, warehousing, and exporting U.S. goods or merchandise. See, e.g., Article II (1) (c), U.S.-Swiss Treaty; Article 5.4(d), U.S. draft model treaty (1981).

105. § 864(c)(4)(b).

106. § 864(c)(4)(iii).

107. On the other hand, a foreign office is not considered to participate materially in a sale merely because: (i) the sale is made subject to the final approval of such an office; (ii) the property sold is distributed from the foreign office; (iii) the foreign office is used for the purpose of having title to the property pass outside of the Unites States; or (iv) the foreign office performs merely clerical functions incident to the sale. [Treasury Reg. § 1.864-6(b)(3)(1).]

108. The current U.S.-Antilles Treaty has an identical provision, but this provision undoubtedly will be dropped in the treaty expected to be signed by June 30, 1984.

109. Sam Siegel, 45 T.C. 566 (1966), acq., 1966-2 C.B. 7.

110. The Act originally was introduced four years ago. Before its final enactment, it had undergone numerous changes, including the last-minute inclusion of the compromise provisions of Title IV which directly affect the applicability of antitrust laws to export trade activities.

For a thorough discussion of the applicable laws prior to the Act (such as the Webb-Pomerene Act), a background on the legislative process up to the summer of 1982, and an explanation of the significant policy changes in export trade activities and the separation of banking and commerce functions that the Act represents, see Reinsch, "The Export Trading Company Act of 1981," *Law and Policy in International Business* 14 (1982): 47.

111. A Chase Econometrics study reportedly has projected that the trade activities spurred by the Act will create up to 640,000 new jobs by 1985.

112. The Act expressly amends the Federal Trade Commission Act, § 5 and adds a new section (§ 7) to the Sherman Act. It does not, however, make any change in the Clayton Act, including § 7, and, for this reason reliance on Title IV of the Act may not provide equivalent protection to certification under Title III of the Act.

113. Note, however, that the Act may present some confusing definitional problems because the same term is defined under different titles of the Act and is sometimes defined differently. For examples, "export trade" is defined in both §§ 103 and 311, "services" is defined in §§ 103 and 311, and "export trade services" is defined in §§ 103 and 203. In addition, the purposes of different titles of the Act are given in §§ 102, 201, and 301.

114. "Services" includes, but is not limited to, a list of professional activities including accounting, automatic data processing, consulting, legal, management, and transportation services [§ 103(a)(2); also, see § 311].

115. "Export trade services" include, but are not limited to, consulting, international market research, advertising, marketing, insurance, product research and design, legal assistance, transportation, including trade documentation and freight forwarding, communication and processing of foreign orders to and for exporters and foreign purchasers, warehousing, foreign exchange, financing and taking title to goods, when provided in order to facilitate the export of goods or services produced in the United States [§ 103(3)].

116. In determining whether or how to structure an ETC, these factors should be considered: (1) produce market, (2) geographic market, (3) investors and percentage of equity, (4) complexity of anticipated transactions, (5) whether ETC will have only one client or many clients, and (6) range of services.

117. See Kermit W. Almstedt, "The Export Trading Company Act—Banking on an Old Idea," *The China Business Review* (Jan.-Feb. 1982); *Export Trading Companies, Trade Associations, and Trade Services*, Senate Report of the Comm. on Banking, Housing and Urban Affairs, #97-27, March 17, 1981, 13-14.

118. An "export trading company" in which these banking-affiliated institutions may invest must be "*exclusively* engaged in activities related to international trade." This is an additional requirement not included in the definition of an ETC which is not bank affiliated. These non-bank-affiliated ETCs need only engage "principally" in U.S. export trade.

119. Conference Report on § 734, "Export Trading Company Act of 1982" and Conferees Explanatory Statement on Bill Passed by Congress and Sent to President on October 1, 1982; Conferees' Statements Under Title II, Bankers Acceptances.

120. Only an enjoinment is authorized if the "national interest" is threatened.

121. The statute of limitations is two years from discovery of noncompliance or four years from when the "action accrues."

122. For example, the legislative history states that there must be effect on domestic commerce, or on the export commerce of a U.S. resident. (Conference Report and Conferees' Explanatory Statement Sent to President on October 1, 1982). The express language of the title, however, does not specify U.S. resident but rather refers to persons "engaged in . . . commerce in the United States."

123. Moore, "Late Addition May Prove To Be Key to Export Act," *Legal Times* (October 11, 1982): 1.

7

FINANCING AND COLLECTIONS

INTRODUCTION TO FINANCING EXPORTS

There are many ways to finance exports. Among these methods, one can tailor financing to one's products, markets, and buyers' needs worldwide.

An exporter may want to merely continue with its own commercial bank with which it has a good working relationship and will give it the best rates; or it may want to consider a government agency. Agencies of the U.S. government will help an exporter find buyers for its products and will facilitate (in cooperation with commercial banks) financing its sales. These agencies will also provide protection against political and commercial risks. Banks can obtain credit information on foreign buyers. Financing is usually done through letters of credit, open account, or draft collection terms. The U.S. Department of Commerce has information on thousands of buyers worldwide. Dun and Bradstreet, a private credit institution, has an international service.

To finance exports, an exporter may use its own working capital or bank lines of credit. A wide variety of financing institutions provide international financing and marketing assistance to exporters. About 250 U.S. banks have qualified international departments. Larger banks have correspondent relationships with banks in most foreign countries or have their own overseas branches. Factoring houses deal in accounts receivable of U.S. exports. They may charge higher fees, but may also purchase receivables without recourse, giving immediate payment on export sales.

Some Export Management Companies (EMCs) also will finance export sales, giving prompt payment and eliminating foreign credit risks. Finally, the U.S. government finances U.S. exports. Eximbank offers direct loans (long-term financing), cooperating with commercial banks (in the United States and abroad) to help U.S. exporters offer credit to overseas buyers.

SOME METHODS

Export Letters of Credit

The buyer arranges for his local bank to issue a letter of credit in favor of the seller (after the sales contract is made). The buyer's bank asks its correspondent bank in the United States to notify the seller that the letter of credit is established, and outlines terms and conditions of the letter of credit.

In a letter of credit in "irrevocable" form, issued by the buyer's bank and confirmed by a U.S. bank, credit risk is virtually eliminated for the U.S. seller; it also protects the foreign buyer in that the U.S. bank will only pay the seller when terms and conditions of the letter of credit are met. Letter of credit financing can be expensive for a buyer: some governments require deposits, and bank fees are charged to establish the letters of credit. A letter of credit that calls for a time draft (60-90 days after its date) and banker's acceptance may be a means for the buyer to obtain credit in the United States while the seller still receives cash from his sale immediately.

Open Account

When dealing with established buyers, or when a sale is to an exporter's own subsidiaries, open account is the simplest method—no letters of credit, no documents, and no bank charges are involved. However, the exporter in this case bears the total risk of collection.

Drafts (on Foreign Buyers): "Sight" or "Time" Drafts

In this case the seller takes shipping documents and its own draft to his bank; the U.S. bank forwards the documents and draft to its correspondent bank (nearest buyer), and *that* bank notifies the buyer that the documents have arrived. The buyer can only claim the documents and title to the goods when he pays and/or sights the draft ("sight draft, documents against payments [s/d, d/p]"). With a time draft, the buyer commits himself to pay it at maturity, at some future date, either from the date of the draft or from the point of "sighting" the draft. A list of possible financing sources for U.S. exports and investments is shown in Exhibit 7.1.

Export Financing

Six U.S. agencies are now active in overseas sales financing: the Export-Import Bank, the Small Business Administration, the Commodity Credit Corporation, the Agency for International Development, the Overseas Private Investment Corporation, and the Department of Commerce Trade and Development Program.

These programs, which in the aggregate support the export of many billions of dollars worth of U.S. goods each year, have been devised for varying purposes. In the case of the Eximbank, for example, boosting U.S. exports is a primary objective, while the focus of the Agency for International Development has been to stimulate economic development in Third World nations. The Overseas Private Investment Corporation and the Trade and Development Program have pursued the dual purpose of stimulating both Third World development and U.S. exports.

THE EXPORT-IMPORT BANK

The Export-Import Bank has been the major source of U.S. government credit for U.S. exporters. In recent years, the Export-Import Bank has devoted an increasing percentage of its resources to supporting exports to developing countries, reflecting in part their greater need for credit with which to purchase goods and services.

The Eximbank supports exports through three major financing programs. First is its direct credit facility, used to finance products and projects requiring long-term repayment periods, ranging from 5 to 15 years. These items include large mining, industrial, and infrastructure projects, as well as products such as commercial jet aircraft. The Eximbank reviews its direct credit interest rate periodically to adjust it to current market conditions and the rates offered by comparable institutions in other exporting nations.

The second major Eximbank program is its bank guarantees and export credit insurance operations. Commercial bank guarantees assure repayment to U.S. banks engaged in financing U.S. exports on medium-term (in the 181 days to 5-year range). Eximbank now maintains relations with a network of over 300 U.S. commercial banks for the joint conduct of this program. The U.S. exporter is able to deal directly

Exhibit 7.1 International Payment Terms

Method	Usual Time of Payment	Goods Available to Buyer	Risk to Exporter	Risk to Importer
1. cash in advance	prior to shipment	after payment is made	minimal	relies on exporter to perform as agreed. Maximum risk.
2. letter of credit: confirmed	after shipment made and documents presented to bank	after payment is made	depends on letter of credit (terms)	relies upon exporter to ship the goods described in documents
unconfirmed	same	same	small depending upon status of issuing bank	same
3. documentary collections:				
sight draft, documents against payment (D/P)	upon presentation of draft to buyer	after payment to importer's bank	if draft dishonored, goods are returned	same, unless buyer can inspect goods before payment
time draft, documents against acceptance (D/A)	upon maturity of draft	before payment, after acceptance	buyer must honor draft upon presentation	same
4. open account (most risk)	per agreement, by invoice	before payment	relies on buyer to pay account as agreed	none

with his own commercial bank whose efforts are supported indirectly by the U.S. agency.

Closely related is the Eximbank export credit insurance program operated jointly with the Foreign Credit Insurance Association (FCIA), a New York based group of over 50 major marine and casualty insurance companies that have put together a large pool of capital to bank U.S. export credit requirements. The FCIA works together with U.S. exporters in insuring repayment on their own extension of financing to foreign buyers. FCIA programs are available for both short- and medium-term financing. Rates are determined by the spread of risk involved in the nations to which each exporter is shipping. An important advantage of an FCIA credit insurance policy is that the policy can be assigned to a commercial bank, thereby making it easier for exporters to obtain financing.

The third Eximbank program is its discount loan facility, which makes it possible for U.S. commercial banks to extend fixed-rate export credits. A commercial bank is able to borrow from Eximbank 85 percent of the amount of a fixed-rate loan it has extended to a foreign buyer of U.S. exports. This program is especially attractive to foreign government buyers who frequently prefer fixed-rate credits.

THE SMALL BUSINESS ADMINISTRATION

The Small Business Administration (SBA) has become increasingly involved in export expansion activities in recent years, and has developed a special export revolving line of credit.

The revolving line of credit is available for developing foreign markets and for pre-export financing. It is offered only as a Small Business Administration guaranteed loan issued by a private lending institution to a company that otherwise qualifies for SBA financing. The firms that are eligible to apply for these credits must have been in operation for at least 12 full months prior to filing an application.

The proceeds of a revolving line of credit are available only for specified export market development activities and to finance labor and materials for pre-export production. Professional export marketing advice or services, foreign business travel, or participation in overseas trade shows are examples of eligible expenses to develop a foreign market. On the other hand, the cost of acquiring fixed assets needed to produce exportable products, renting an office or commercial space in a foreign country, equipping such an office, or wages for a staff in such an office are regarded as examples of inappropriate uses of proceeds.

The SBA revolving line cannot exceed more than 18 months, including all extensions and renewals. Acceptable collateral for these credits will be limited to items located in the United States, its territories, and possessions. Collateral may include such items as bank letters of credit, insured receivables (normally by the Foreign Credit Insurance Association), or any other assets under the jurisdiction of U.S. courts.

THE COMMODITY CREDIT CORPORATION

The Commodity Credit Corporation (CCC), an agency of the U.S. Department of Agriculture, makes available a commercial export credit guarantee program for farm product sales in conjunction with the Agriculture Department's Foreign Agriculture Service. In addition, the Agriculture Department operates the Food for Peace P.L. 480 program, a major part of which provides concessional export financing.

The CCC Export Credit Guarantee Program (GSM-102) is designed to expand U.S. agricultural exports by stimulating U.S. bank financing of foreign purchases on credit terms of up to three years. The program operates in cases where credit is necessary to increase or maintain U.S. exports to foreign markets and where financial institutions would be unwilling to provide financing without CCC's guarantee.

Private U.S. banks provide the day-to-day operating funds in these programs. The banks thus profit from their lending, while for exporters the guarantee programs make it easier to locate bank financing and to meet credit competition from other exporting countries.

AGENCY FOR INTERNATIONAL DEVELOPMENT

The U.S. Agency for International Development (AID) provides loans and grants to Third World nations for both developmental and foreign policy reasons. Development loans are extended to support recipient country development plans in certain key economic sectors, especially agriculture and nutrition, health, training and education, and energy. Foreign policy loans under the so-called Economic Support Fund (ESF) are extended to developing countries that face internal or external political and economic instability. These credits are used primarily for balance of payments purposes, to sustain the level of imports needed to run their economies, or for direct budgetary requirements. In both cases — development programs and ESF requirements — a significant portion of each loan or grant is used to finance U.S. exports.

THE OVERSEAS PRIVATE INVESTMENT CORPORATION

The U.S. Overseas Private Investment Corporation (OPIC) is engaged in encouraging U.S. direct investments in developing countries through the provision of political risk insurance and financing services. In recent years, OPIC has attempted, wherever possible, to stimulate U.S. exports through its various programs.

OPIC programs provide financing for U.S. exports in three ways. First, many individual projects require the export of U.S. capital equipment and other products, which are financed by the agency through its own direct lending and through guarantees on bank credits. Second, some OPIC-supported projects create a market for continuing exports of U.S. goods. Third, two relatively new OPIC programs are focused directly on exports: the distributorship program and the leasing program.

The OPIC distributorship program supports the strengthening of foreign distributors that buy U.S. products. OPIC provides direct credits and guarantees of bank loans with long-term repayment schedules, frequently five to eight years. These loans are primarily for physical expansion of the foreign distributor's facilities. OPIC requires that the U.S. exporter share in the financing. In some cases, the overseas distributors are independent firms, while in other cases they are subsidiaries or affiliates of the U.S. exporters.

OPIC's leasing program, recently established, provides loans and guarantees on four-to-five-year terms to overseas leasing firms that are either U.S. owned or have U.S. management. The foreign firms buy U.S. equipment for leasing within their countries and regions.

THE TRADE AND DEVELOPMENT PROGRAM

The Trade and Development Program (TDP) has financed planning services for major development projects in more than 40 different countries over the past several years. The TDP furnishes feasibility studies and other project-planning services, usually on a grant basis. This program only supports those overseas development projects that offer a strong likelihood of future U.S. exports.

The TDP finances a variety of planning services, including definitional studies, which involve small teams of experts at the early "idea stage" of project development, prefeasibility studies, which include preliminary technical, economic, and financial analyses to assess whether projects should be undertaken, and feasibility studies, which offer detailed technical, economic, and financial data required for final decision on whether to proceed with project implementation. Thus, this program finances services directly and stimulates exports of products indirectly through its support for project development.

Exhibit 7.2   Summary of Export Financing Possibilities

1. Export-Import Bank (EXIM) and PEFCO
2. Foreign Credit Insurance Association (FCIA)
3. Agency for International Development (AID)
4. Overseas Private Investment Corporation (OPIC)
5. Department of Agriculture: PL 480–Food for Peace Commodity Credit Corporation (CCC)
6. World Bank Group:
    International Bank for Reconstruction and Development (IBRD)
    International Development Association (IDA)
    International Finance Corporation (IFC)
7. Inter-American Development Bank (IADB)
8. Asian Development Bank (ADB)
9. African Development Fund (ADF)

Other possible sources of funds:

10. Private investment bankers (Chase International Investment Corporation, etc.)
11. Borrowing dollars or other currencies in free markets from foreign banks for use in third markets
12. Local development banks
13. Foreign commercial banks
14. The European Investment Bank (EIB): major source for investments in the common market
15. Local insurance companies and pension funds (against mortgage, collateral)
16. Local wealthy families, trusts, colleges, and churches
17. Government grants or loans at subsidized rates, offered in underdeveloped countries
18. Leasing and leaseback (firm builds its own plant, sells it to a leasing firm, then leases it back)
19. Delayed payment terms from local suppliers
20. Discounting or using as collateral foreign government contracts

---

8

PEOPLE PROBLEMS ABROAD

INTRODUCTION

Human behavior occurs with reference to words, sounds, and signs which represent things or people. Some people like Democracy and hate Communism, enjoy Bach and hate jazz. Some people like olives; others do not. All people either like or dislike all things, including people, to some degree; this is called attitude. In the extreme, it is called prejudice. Just as we seldom find chemical elements existing alone, the elements of behavior usually are found in compounds. Certain combinations recur frequently, probably as a result of standardized tradition and the like. Such combinations differentiate peoples and societies.

Rather than try to change people's behavior or to even complain about it, it is better to capitalize on knowledge of what it is natural for others to do, feel, and believe. This specific knowledge then can be used to advantage in creating a climate that permits an opportunity for each to develop his resources to the fullest extent.

Be flexible. As the "foreigner" abroad, the U.S. exporter should establish itself as a good partner and welcome guest of the country in which it locates an office. This is not just a question of putting out fires during emergencies, but has the positive purpose of being able to do a continuing business and to sell more goods or services.

WHY ADAPT

Certain conditions and circumstances necessitate such a flexible attitude abroad in far greater measure than here at home. First, motives of U.S. companies frequently are suspect because of growing national-ism. Second, there is a lack of appreciation of the social responsibility now accepted as an essential part and practice of U.S. corporate life. Third, every move a company makes abroad affects some key group upon which its success and welfare depend: the government, local civil officials, labor leaders, its own employees, its suppliers, competi-tors, and customers. Finally, each country is different in its national customs, taboos, prejudices, and, of course, pride. Thus, it is incum-bent on U.S. companies to be highly sensitive and adaptable to the local psychology and methodology of doing business.

The Overseas Executive

Since business is not conducted in a vacuum, let us turn our attention for a moment to the overseas sales executive. It is at the executive level that a U.S. company's absorption into the foreign local commu-nity must be effected. One of the most difficult jobs an American executive abroad must do is to share the social interests of his local counterpart. This calls for discipline and effort because we are accus-tomed to separate the office from our social lives.

Americans abroad tend to limit their extracurricular circle of con-tacts only to other Americans, for it is naturally easier for one to relax with people whose cultural background and language are the same as his or her own. This limitation immediately causes local suspicions of our arrogance, indifference, or actual dislike of the people in whose country we live. An American executive abroad and his wife must diligently try to know their native social equals.

Most foreigners do not give their friendship easily, although they accept social advances with courtesy. Such restrained acceptance may discourage an American accustomed to our relaxed manners, but the breakthrough into real friendship creates a relationship based upon deeper personal loyalty than our easy ways usually signify.

Staffing with Nationals

Furthermore, U.S. companies move far toward improving the U.S. image overseas when they open the executive area to local talent. Many international companies draw upon local executives because they can be paid in local currency and will not have to be replaced, unlike the American who returns home eventually.

The decision to appoint local executives, however, often has been a wise one poorly implemented. Local managers are conscious of discrimination just when they are at the height of their working power and influence in the local community. These usually are the most capable, best trained men in the country. To manage or compensate them otherwise is a serious mistake. Yet one point that frequently causes resentment is that many local executives, although paid above the local rate, are paid less than their American counterparts. Furthermore, the local executive knows he is paid less than the man he may have replaced, with no prospect of approaching that salary range.

Customs and Pitfalls

In many areas of the world a person is examined more closely than the business proposition, for it is believed that if the proposition is sensible, then its chances for success rest upon the reliability and competence of the people involved. In failing to understand this because of our intrinsic belief in business as a legitimate activity and in law as a dependable framework for it, it is easy to become offended if a foreigner regards us with suspicion—just as he regards his own compatriots until he knows them well. We often expect an immediate trust and confidence which a foreigner is not prepared to grant. Thus, to him, our resultant aggrieved reactions are either arrogant or naive (or both), neither of which is a very acceptable one.

Marketers overseas may unwittingly violate taboos, whether cultural, religious, or political. Blue, for example, is a mourning color in Iran and is not favorably received in commercial products. Green, the nationalistic color of Egypt and Syria, is frowned upon for use in packages. Showing pairs of anything in West Africa is disapproved of. White is the color of mourning in Japan and unpopular in products. Brown and gray are disapproved of in Nicaragua. Purple is generally unwelcome in most Latin American markets because of its association with death. In Thailand, any object or package showing feet is likely to be offensive.

Food is a problem. Brahmans are vegetarians; Muslims or Orthodox Jews avoid pork in any form; Buddhists will not drink alcoholic beverages. In many Middle and Far Eastern countries, food is not passed or eaten with the left hand because the left hand is used for bodily functions. In addition, an attitude of personal restraint will carry one much farther than the customary American levity and good cheer. Generally, a smile opens doors—a laugh opens exits.

In matters of clothing, an African woman might walk a street with her breasts bare, yet be shocked to see an American woman in toreador pants. In contrast, in many Asian lands, women wear hip-clinging dresses slit to the upper mid-thigh, yet would never expose their breasts or shoulders. Thus, what is proper or improper depends on the situation and local customs; Americans should not judge dress or habits of other cultures by our standards.

Business Considerations

In technical training, become familiar with the way business is conducted in the country. Do not become exasperated when you find it takes two days of personal consultations to accomplish abroad what one three-minute telephone call might do at home. Learn to enjoy the challenge of doing business in new ways, with new hazards, but with the potentiality of new rewards.

While Americans are taught to revere equality, to distrust elaborate formality, and to uphold clear thinking, many other people operate from quite different premises. Clarity and logic are less appreciated in some societies than they are in the United States, while equality is often held to be a social vice rather than a virtue.

Foreign Viewpoint

In addition to lack of preparedness in the cultural amenities, equally destructive are superficial judgment of foreign operations. Foreign managers are inclined to think about problems in great depth. They often maintain a subtle and delicate balance of power and conduct many affairs on a highly personalized basis. To an American, with limited exposure, these actions may seem essentially wrong, and he is apt to externalize his feelings without sufficiently understanding the reasons for them. Such actions tend to confirm overseas impressions of the American prototype as being rather insensitive and shallow.

To complicate matters further, foreign managers may make major capital investments in facilities and equipment that cannot be justified rationally on the basis of projected sales volume or of foreseeable return on investment. The decision may be made on the basis of added personal prestige the investment produces in the industrial community, or the notion that "we should be in the field," or simply that the investment will provide more employment.

Thus, we are tested continually on our deftness in maintaining patience, convincing others in their language rather than our own, and our perceptiveness in appreciating other viewpoints. To think not only in terms of the language of a country, but in terms of its traditions, customs, and ethics, entails gaining sufficient exposure to realize the relativity of our own particular values.

Building Staff

What kind of people do we need to cope with all the foregoing situations? Building an international staff always entails "people problems," in addition to problems of money and time. If handled properly, these factors can combine to create a situation characterized by deep reward and satisfaction for all concerned, both local people and expatriate alike.

In building its international staff, an exporter should consider four basic points: (1) the person—his qualifications and viewpoint; (2) training—what kind and how much; (3) compensation and benefits, including the physical movement and handling of the employee and his family; (4) the pitfalls of doing business abroad or the web of custom and culture confronting a person and his family living and doing business overseas.

There are two aspects to the relationship between American business and its personnel abroad: (1) the commitment the employee makes by going abroad and (2) the investment the company makes in sending him abroad.

There is another subtle dimension to consider which is the American assumption that business is an honorable undertaking. In many countries, in fact, businessmen have little or no social standing, and scholars, military leaders, and politicians are accorded far more status and position in the cultural scheme. Our expatriates must recognize, understand, and accept this situation where it may exist.

What to Look For

Five general elements seem relevant to effective overseas performance; consider these points in staffing: (1) technical skill; (2) belief in mission or job assignment; (3) cultural empathy; (4) political sense; (5) organization ability.

To translate the above into specifics, look for people with the following traits:

1. Resourcefulness—those who snap back rapidly from discouragement and frustration.

2. Environmental mobility, suggesting exposure to many kinds of people. Give special consideration to those demonstrating a spirit of adventure, an eye to far-off places, and the capacity to weather new experiences.

3. Intellectual curiosity and a disposition for learning new things.

4. "Institution building"—those with varied interests, i.e., managing a club, committee work in community activities, sports, and other similar activities.

A wrong decision may be costly and fraught with repercussions. Foreign posts demand unique managerial talents. Training should include enough exposure to foreign ways to realize the relativity of our own values. Look for those with a talent for combining personnel and other resources into self-sustaining enterprises, an ability to utilize skills and forces to make the desired happen. Careful pursuit of the foregoing principles can assist an exporter immeasurably in achieving success.

INDEX

ABOUT THE AUTHORS

Dr. R. Duane Hall has served as officer in and consultant to various multinational corporations and has personally conducted corporate and consultancy engagements throughout Western Europe, Thailand, Singapore, Taiwan, Mexico, and Japan. He has been a corporate speaker/lecturer at international meetings in Mexico, Taiwan, Thailand, Republic of South Africa, Japan, and throughout the United States for the American Management Association and other organizations. Professional affiliations include: The American Management Association, National Association of Corporate Directors, and as a member of the U.S. Department of Commerce Export Council for Arizona. His major fields of competency include: Multinational Marketing Strategies and Planning, International Trade Operations, Corporate Strategic Planning, Overseas Joint Ventures, and Global Corporate Governance. He serves periodically as a professional "outside director" for international firms. His first book, *International Trade Operations: A Managerial Approach*, was published in late 1983. His second book, *The International Joint Venture*, was published in November 1984.

Mr. Ralph Gilbert, Esquire, a partner of Baker & McKenzie, is a graduate of the United States Naval Academy at Annapolis, B.S. 1951 (with distinction); Georgetown University Law School, LL.B. 1957 (Editor Law Review); and the Harvard Business School, M.B.A. 1960. He specializes in international trade and investment law, with emphasis on export strategy, tax planning, licensing, joint ventures, and direct investment abroad.

Prior to joining Baker & McKenzie in 1965, Mr. Gilbert served as a Nuclear Officer, Joint Armed Forces Special Weapons Project, 1951-54; a Fellow at the Institute for Foreign and International Trade Law, Goethe University, Frankfurt, Germany, 1957-58; and legal counsel for the Amerada Petroleum–Continental Oil–Marathon Oil operating consortium in Tripoli, Libya, 1961-64. He is a frequent lecturer on international trade and tax issues at the World Trade Institute, the American Management Association, and at various trade associations and universities.

Mr. Gilbert is a member of the New York and Illinois Bars, American Bar Association, International Bar Association, Chicago Association of Commerce and Industry (Export Policy Committee), the Mid-America Committee, and the Chicago Economic Club.